METAMORPHOSIS

Kevin Childs

'For Aaron, the wisest and most beautiful
person I know, with all my love'

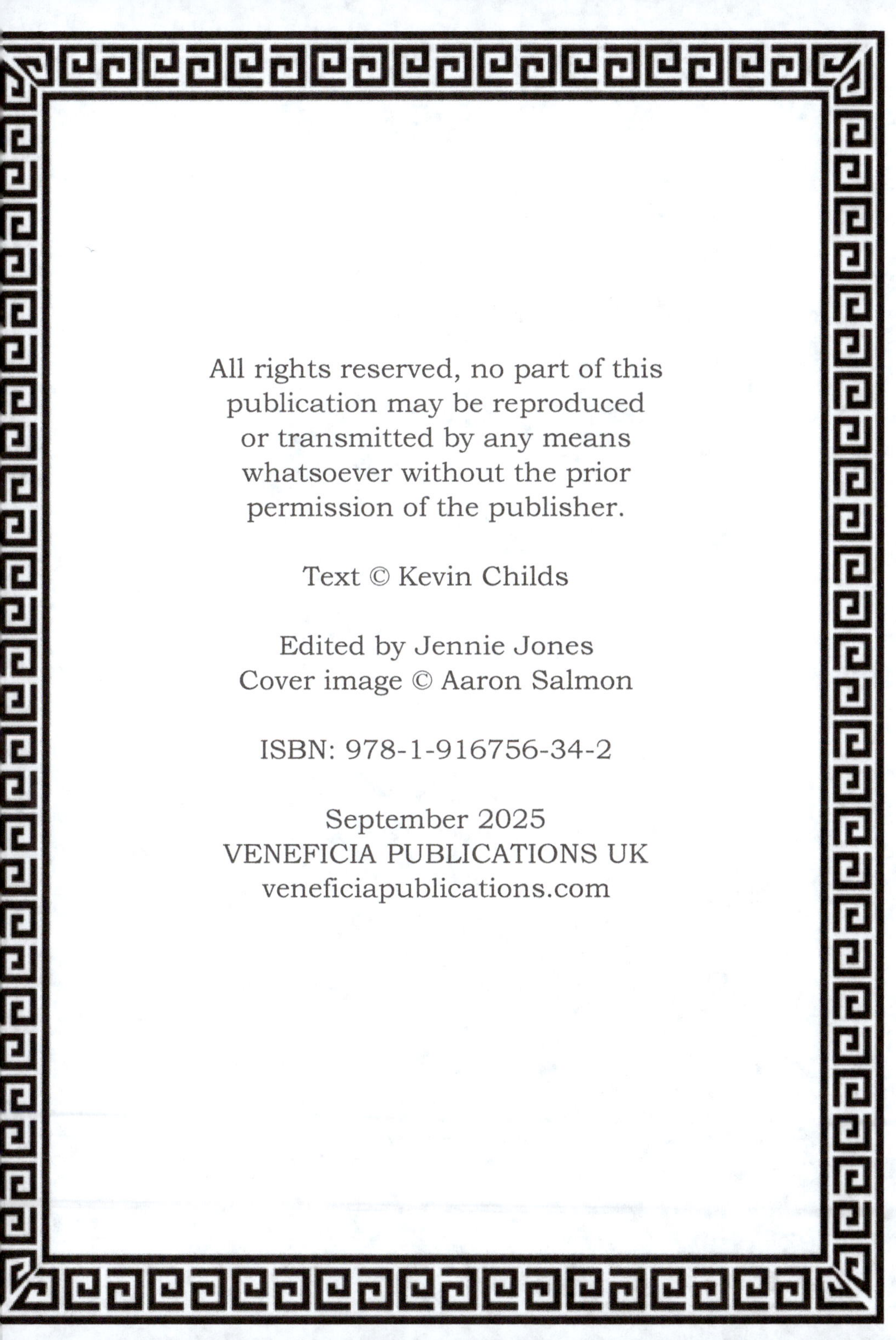

Text © Kevin Childs

Edited by Jennie Jones
Cover image © Aaron Salmon

ISBN: 978-1-916756-34-2

September 2025
VENEFICIA PUBLICATIONS UK
veneficiapublications.com

CONTENTS

INTRODUCTION

In September 2021, my partner of nearly thirty years died suddenly. We were visiting some friends in Scotland. The day we arrived, Jonathan had cycled around the local loch with our dog, Molly, and I had followed behind, struggling to keep up over the rocky road. His strength and resilience were always remarkable.

The following morning, some of us set off for a long walk through an enchanted wood full of brightly-coloured mosses, mushrooms and toadstools. The weather was cool and a little damp. Jonathan went on ahead and then waited for us on a bench overlooking the loch. We scrambled down to the road and climbed through the tangle of a path-less pine wood to a little beach on the loch itself. We'd brought sandwiches and drinks, and we sat and ate while chatting about the beauty of the place and watching Molly charging into the water after various sticks. Then we set off back to the house through the woods, taking a different path. We hadn't gone more than a hundred metres or so when Jonathan, walking just ahead of me, suddenly fell to the ground. I didn't know it then, but he died almost immediately from a devastating narrowing of the main artery into his heart, a condition he had no idea of, and which had produced no symptoms until that moment. Silent ischaemic heart disease.

I still find it difficult to fathom how this could have happened. For nearly two hours we tried CPR to revive him until the air ambulance was able to find us and land in a clearing in the woods surrounding us. It had started to rain softly, and the midges had come out, although I hardly noticed as I cradled Jonathan in my lap and sang to him.

The months following were like an appalling dream I just couldn't wake from. Often, I felt as though I was watching myself go through the residue of living, struggling to cope with a drastically reduced income, wandering from one room to another in an empty house. I would sit alone or lie on the bed for hours, my hand stroking Molly's head. Or I would force myself to take her on the walks we'd shared: every tree, every path and field keenly cutting me with the blade of memory.

I wanted to leave the house and our life in Devon but couldn't bring myself to. I had loved him so very much for so very long. I hoped something of him lingered in the place. And from time to time, I could still feel him, his presence just out of sight in another room, on the stairs, once even in our bed.

Jonathan was a well-known human rights lawyer. He'd given so much of his time to the organisations and people he helped. Everyone wanted to grieve with me, so finally I was able to organise a suitable memorial for him with the help of his old Chambers, Doughty Street in London. It kept me going. To see so many people from all over the world coming together to celebrate him was humbling. Afterwards I felt very empty, a hollow man, eating and speaking but without any purpose or conviction. Friends and family began to move on, understandably. I remained in a dark place wishing I were dead, that I'd fallen down that September day, that the sea would swallow me, or the earth bury me.

Then one evening I went down to a beach near where I live and watched the moon rise over the sea, and I prayed for the first time in years – not to the Christian god I'd rejected when I was a gay teenager growing up in a Catholic household, not to any specific deity but to whatever numinous presence filled the void. And that night, I dreamed for the first time in months. I saw, as clear as the night sky, a preternaturally beautiful woman walking the moonlit path on the sea and what I experienced was both a vision of her and, perhaps, something I remembered from reading. [1]

My own personal image of Isis, the great mother of all, was vivid and real. And my journey began in that dream, a dream which is a sort of prologue to this collection.

While I didn't intend to publish most of the poetry in this collection, the circumstances that I've described brought this book about – events which were out of

---

1. I have been struck by the similarity of my dream to a passage in The Golden Ass by the second-century Roman author Apuleius. I hadn't read it for thirty years, but my vision was as clear as his.

my control but of which, with hindsight, I seem to have had some sort of prescience. Several of the poems I've included here are predictions, or more properly, premonitions of the overwhelming events which set me on a journey to the now, although they were written between ten and twenty years ago.

I decided to publish these poems partly because I thought it might help others who find themselves in a similar place of grief and partly because I wanted to explore my own journey to a new understanding of the world in which we live.

I am a pagan. I believe that the natural world is infused with a spiritual quality that demands respect and understanding.

It's a bit of a cliché these days to say that our civilisation has lost that understanding, leading to the devastating exploitation of the landscapes we have inherited and helped mould over thousands of years. We've lost that sense of numinous wonder in every rock and tree and animal. They've become simple consumables.

But every spirit that inhabits them, every god and goddess whose names have been various over the centuries, and every daemon of the woods and mountains and seas cries out against us.

I also have my own personal reasons for embracing the style of paganism that I follow, and those reasons have dictated the choice of some of the poems included in this collection.

I have called this collection '*Metamorphosis*' because of the old belief that the universe is governed by flux. Everything is in a state of decay and renewal. Atoms transform into new matter. Metamorphosis occurs at every moment. We grow and age and die and throughout that process we are constantly changing from one form of ourselves to another. In his terrifying image of the Last Judgement, the artist Michelangelo depicted himself in the crumpled skin of Saint Bartholomew. As he gazes at the shining, beardless divinity at the centre of all this, no longer the Son of God but the Sun God, Bartholomew seems about to discard his old self. He is in his perfected body after all, heroic, godlike. I too am no longer what

I was, and yet I cling to my old self even while I look on the divine. So, this collection isn't just a journey, it charts a process of transformation, or metamorphosis.

Looking back at my older poems, written over the last twenty years or so, I was struck by how much I seemed to understand of this. It was only an apprehension, but I always knew that moment in the Scottish woods might happen, that death would rob me of my peace, and of love.

My more recent poems, written during 2022 and 2023, often came from a place of darkness or despair, but also through a sweet awakening, which taught me that creativity is a means to living in the night. We're all dying every day, from the moment we're born; a slow, inevitable creeping towards an end which might be equally slow or shockingly sudden. We can never really predict this. But we can predict the sense of it. A passage in Homer's epic poem of the Trojan War, *The Iliad*, has the great warrior Achilles laughing at a Trojan prince who begs for his life:

Look at me, how big and fine I am, my father's a great man, and a goddess bore me, yet death and remorseless fate await me too, either at sunrise, evening or high noon, some man in battle will strike me with his spear or pierce me with an arrow from his bow. [2]

To mitigate what we intuit of our fate we have love, a gift that is as much a place of creativity as the darkness that sometimes threatens to suffocate us.

I have always been fascinated by Greek paganism and the myths surrounding it.

Like many in the Western world, I was brought up on the Greek and Roman classics, the stories told by Homer and Hesiod, Ovid and Virgil. To explain the world in which they lived through stories was, to my mind, the Greeks' greatest contribution to civilisation. Not the philosophies of Plato or Aristotle, who were too in love with notions of what they could see or touch or taste, an empiricism that

---

2. Homer The Iliad 21.110. The translations from Latin and Greek in this introduction are the author's own.

reduced everything to an atom, but the retelling of those stories by Aeschylus and Euripides and all the other poets of the pagan world. To know that everything is holy, unknowable but in a state of symbiosis with everything else is to begin truly to see and feel and taste. There is magic in a blade of grass, or a reed or a laurel tree because it was made so by its own sacredness.

Hesiod, perhaps the original collator of many of the myths we now know, described how the earth goddess Gaia gave birth to thousands of divine beings who cared for and haunted the woods and rivers and seas:

...there are, amongst the myriad of others, three thousand gentle-footed daughters of Ocean scattered far and wide, bright children among the goddesses, and all alike look after the earth and the depths of the standing water.[3]

I don't agree with much that the English poet Robert Graves wrote about

---

3.   Hesiod, Theogony 365

his own paganism, but I do think he was onto something when he condemned the Athenian philosopher Socrates for his rejection of myth, calling him: "A confirmed townsman who seldom visited the countryside." Among other things, Socrates had once said "fields and trees will not teach me anything, but men do."[4] It's a sad aphorism, for we know nothing of what the trees know, so it's no surprise that Plato, Socrates's pupil, had his master banish poetic myth from the ideal body politic in The Republic.

I also recognise that my Grecocentric paganism is only a reflection of what more ancient traditions can teach us. The Greeks learned from the Egyptians, and the Egyptians, perhaps, from the Sumerians, but the Greeks refined what they harvested. Isis, who has played such an important role in my life, was a major goddess among many, for example, before the Greeks and Romans conquered Egypt and then elevated her to the supreme deity of deities, the power of the sun and moon

---

4.   Graves The White Goddess 8

combined, the manifestation of the very cosmos itself.

I am only just beginning to understand the pagan traditions of the north of Europe; the gods and myths of the Celts, Scandinavia and the old Germanic peoples. Even here, it's tempting to adopt an easy syncretism, like the Romans, who enlisted local gods into their own pantheon as an early form of spiritual globalisation. It's why Pan, the supreme nature deity, emerges from so many other woodland gods across the world and is now a master god of modern paganism; partly because he was never one of the canonical Olympian gods, never an inhabitant of the unknowable sky.

This is the hinterland of my beliefs. For a long time, I had rejected any notion of religion and may even have fancied myself an atheist. But life, or the cycle we understand as life and death, has a way of penetrating well-intentioned rationalism. It's through grief, through the darkness that shrouds our rational being whenever things go wrong, that we recognise the limits of the sort of scepticism Hamlet berates Horatio for in Shakespeare's play:

"There are more things in heaven and earth… than are dreamt of in your philosophy."[5]

I have learned to love that darkness through the memory of the warmth of nights spent with a man I met about a year after Jonathan died. I have found it liberating in a way I could never confess or even acknowledge to myself in the past. Jonathan was a creature of light and reason. Like a man of the Enlightenment, he required reasonableness and kindness in himself and in other people. It's why he cared so much about the causes he tried to help, and it's why he was so admired.

But I have always been of the shadows, a child of a chthonic deity, Dionysus to his Apollo, if you like, open to intoxication in every sense. That doesn't make me bad or unreasonable. I just recognise the power and latent potential of darkness, and that it has its own light.

Jonathan refused to recognise this and had little empathy with the chthonic. He could be infuriating towards those closest to him; rational to the point of

---

5.   Shakespeare Hamlet 1.5.167-8

madness. As a result, I was always in his shadow, a place I felt comfortable in for much of the thirty-odd years we were together. And from where I have been dragged into the light by his death.

In August 2022, I visited the southern Peloponnese in Greece with a good friend, and we travelled around looking at ancient ruins and holy places. One trip was to a vast cave system near Diros, which had been inhabited by humans for tens of thousands of years. Multi-coloured limestone stalactites and stalagmites seemed to grow organically along a path through caverns that ran for over five kilometres into the mountainside. In ancient times, this cave system was believed to lead to the Kingdom of Hades.

And like so many other grottoes, it had also become sacred to the god Pan in the early history of the region. Pan is the ultimate god of nature. He has special care of the natural world and those who live and work in it; he can make the crops grow with spring rains or wither in the hot sun, and his voice could strike terror even in the hearts of other gods:

Pan lord of the woodlands and of war, sheltering from the daylight hours in caverns; but about midnight in lonely places those shaggy shanks and fierce horned brow can be seen. Louder than any trumpet sounds his voice, and at that sound veteran warriors drop their swords in fear, the charioteer falls from his careering car and bolts from gates on city walls drop down by night.[6]

If Pan were ever roused from his sleep in these caves, his shout would have echoed through the rock, causing the earth to shake and the cool air to scream in terror. Indeed, in the fourth millennium BCE, it seems the cave entrance collapsed in one such earthquake, trapping hundreds of people inside.

A few miles from Diros, in the hills above the city of Sparta, is an old Mycenaean shrine, built of great blocks of local stone rising to a broad platform on a high promontory. To one side is a palace complex. But from ancient times, the main

---

6.   Valerius Flaccus Argonautica 3.47

structure on the hill was believed to be a tomb in which the bones of the Spartan king Menelaus and his wife Helen were buried. A benign neglect has kept this site free of tourists. Excavations from the 1960s suggest that this was the original city of Sparta, of Homeric legend, but there were no fences, no barriers, no signs of ongoing archaeological work. Just the great blocks of limestone, seemingly carved by giants, that made the foundations of the shrine. Christianity had tried to pollute this spot with a small chapel, but it was insignificant amongst all that ancient pagan grandeur.

And it was between these two locations, one under the ground, the other open to the sky, that I began to think of the structure for a collection of poetry.

Metamorphosis follows my journey into darkness. The first section, 'Epiphaneia' which means "manifestation", is mostly made up of poems I have written since 2004, with some personal reflections on my relationship with Jonathan, and some expressions of anger or frustration at the way people like me – gay men, lesbians, those who don't conform to a heteronormative so-called reality – were treated back in the day (and still are, sadly). I remember that I came to the writing of these through a clear understanding that the pagan world had few prejudices about sex and sexuality. Homophobia is a construct of monotheism, promulgated across the globe through nearly 2,000 years of a warped Christianity. Same-sex intimacy was equated with paganism by the early church, which tried to stamp it out as a mortal sin. As if we could stop being born. And those attitudes persist, even amongst some modern pagans who, like Robert Graves, have a very narrow view of what fertility means, and who see the cycle of life as a simple linear journey. I am with Aleister Crowley when he wrote, 'Do what thou wilt shall be the whole of the Law'.

But this is not the place to evaluate such things. My route to paganism came through my understanding of sexuality, in part at least, as a yearning for union with the great heart of the universe which rejects nothing, and through which nothing that exists can be deemed unnatural. In the second century BCE, the

Roman playwright Terence wrote: "I am a human being. I think nothing human is alien to me." It's why I've also included poems about Mary Magdalen and Jesus's infancy; not for any specifically Christian message, but for their origins in much earlier traditions of the cycle of life.

The 'Five Sonnets (After Michelangelo)', which form a penultimate group within this first section, are partly a manifestation of my obsession as an art historian with Michelangelo's particular genius, and partly a reflection in miniature of the entire journey of *Metamorphosis*.

Michelangelo was a fine poet, as well as a genius of visual media. He was both a child of his time, imbued with the beliefs of late medieval Christianity, and entirely out of his time; a "revenant", as the 19th-century commentator Walter Pater called him, of the old beliefs, a pagan aesthete trying to reconcile the old religion with the new.[7] It is a fascinating journey to a dead end, from which he (and by analogy, I) is saved by love – love, which is both physical and spiritual, love that is all-consuming

---

7.   Pater The Renaissance 54

like a tempering fire, love that dared not speak its name for too much of the five hundred years since his time.

But the core of this first section is an exploration of death, culminating in that wood in Scotland. It is a place of no return for the one whose spirit falls under the earth, but also for those who witness it and are left behind, often unable to move on from the event.

The second section, 'In the Earth', is my journey into the land of the dead. Like the 14th-century Florentine poet, Dante, I have my companions on that journey: the Roman aesthete and writer Petronius, who was forced to commit suicide through the jealousy of the emperor Nero, throwing a dinner party so his friends could witness the act; the 13th-century poet Rumi; the man-god Dionysus in his most enigmatic guise.

These were sexually ambiguous men who celebrated love in all its aspects, and who understood loss profoundly. The section describes winter landscapes of ice and snow, the cold turning of the year, a drowning in the sea, culminating in the annihilation of the ego in divine light through a translation from Dante himself.

The title of the final section I have taken from Dante again. La Vita Nuova, or 'the new life', was his first collection of poems and prose, charting the course of his love for Beatrice Portinari and her early death. It is an examination of the transformational qualities of love, and it seemed pertinent to the new life I have begun after the death of Jonathan and my meeting Aaron in the summer of 2022.

Love and desire, the creational spectre of sex as both the most intense physical energy of love and the obliteration of identity in sensual pleasure, akin to the obliteration of the self in death, are some of the themes I've explored in this new poetry, with the help of Baudelaire and others who went there before me. For example, 'The Mirror' recasts the story of Salome, the stepdaughter of King Herod Antipas, who danced her way into legend as a modern phenomenon of an insane world.

I have also found a new, deeper understanding of the power of pagan beliefs through my dreams and readings of the ancient gods. Myths offer insights into our lives, if we allow them to penetrate the veils we hang about us: the overly rational mindset, the prejudices of our education, and the psychological warping of grief. It's why I've begun this section with the beautiful story of Aphrodite, Goddess of Love, and the 'King of the Frogs', a story of the origin of love, set in a primeval, sacred landscape.

I end the collection with a poem that is a hymn to Pan. The Greeks saw gods as beyond the constraints of being human: capable of rationalism but also closer to the instinct of animals. Their immortality was instinctual, not rational. Pan, part divine humanoid and part literal animal, like many of the gods of ancient Egypt, epitomises that duality. He is a god of the earth and the sea, one whom necromancers would invoke to predict the future. He wasn't worshipped in temples built in cities, but in caves and woods. He is the horned one that Christianity tried to turn into a manifestation of supreme evil. But as the ancients knew long ago, there is no such thing as supreme evil or supreme good. There is only a stirring of passions and insights that can lead all of us, humans and gods, down different paths.

Which brings me back to those mysterious caves leading into the bowels of the earth and that hillside overlooking Sparta in the August of 2022. I had experienced both the underworld thereby, and a conduit to the heavens.

I have been asked how it's possible for me to have moved on from Jonathan's death. The impossibility is not moving on. When I met Aaron, who is the inspiration of so much of what I've written recently, I barely understood that love could be in me again, although my dream of Isis had promised me this. But when I stood with my dear friend, Susan, just outside Sparta by that old shrine of Helen I felt the pang of separation from him keenly and realised that Aaron had crept into my heart and would remain there. Susan had no judgement of me. She is like a muse herself, a wonderful manifestation of the power of place and spirit, elemental. I owe this revelation to our shared love of poking about old ruins. And Aaron has many of the same qualities.

He and Jonathan are like two valves in my heart, a phantom within a crystal, and they are both equally responsible for the writing and collation of these poems. Jonathan is the muse of yesterday, of tragedy and loss. Aaron is the muse of lyrical love poetry and the promise of tomorrow.

I would not be here without that insight. I wouldn't have begun this journey nor had the drive to complete it. I've felt a peace I hadn't experienced for a very long time, not a contentment but a need to follow my instincts and not worry about what others may think.

In *The Odyssey*, Homer describes how Helen, now back in Sparta with her husband Menelaus, drugs the wine he shares with their guests, Odysseus's young son, Telemachus, who is searching for his father, and his companion Peisistratus:

She put a drug into the wine from which they were drinking which frees men from grief and from anger and causes oblivion of all ills. [8]

---

8.   Homer Odyssey 4.219

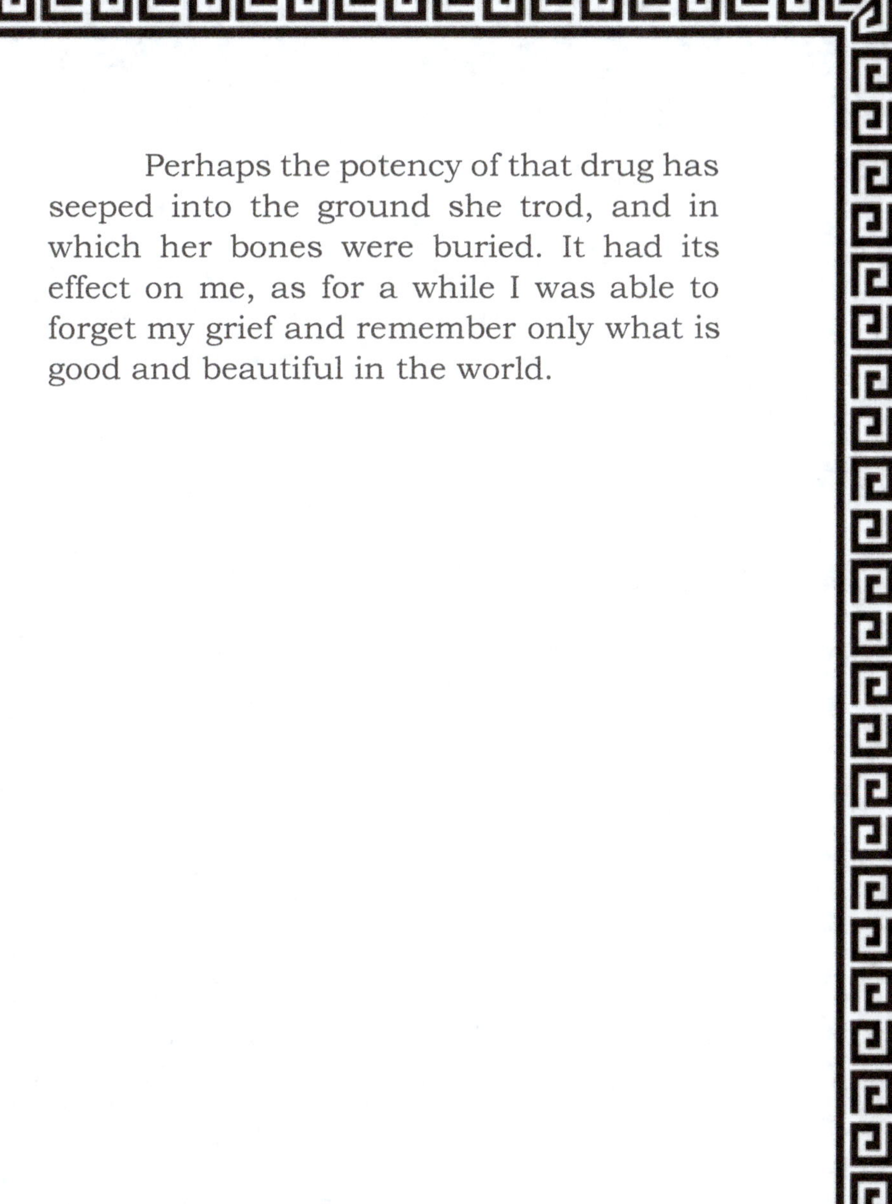

Perhaps the potency of that drug has seeped into the ground she trod, and in which her bones were buried. It had its effect on me, as for a while I was able to forget my grief and remember only what is good and beautiful in the world.

EPIPHANIA

THE PROMISE

So, I stood on the beach that night.
He was gone and I was all alone.
The Milky Way stretched cold, a great fold
Of fabric full of stars, a crescent moon
Breaking the black horizon
Like the horns of a magical beast
Risen from some feast of legend.
A watery path to its silvery cut
In the dark blue heaven.
And I prayed.

I begged to be free of this torment,
For the blood to flow warm again
In my pale veins. For love, for hate,
For feeling to return and burn my arms.
For the cold sweat to be dissolved.
For him. For a new life. For joy
And bitterness. To feel, to steal
That never be nothing again.
And under the dark heaven
I fell down.

The cold sand held me down. My hands
Felt the depth of water within it,
Vast oceans beyond the power
Of the waves. But there was no warmth.
Tears fell, swelled from my black eyes
Down my cheeks onto the black sand.
There was no comfort in the place,
Familiar, hostile. He wasn't there.
And under that dark heaven
I turned back.

That night I dreamt in my cold bed.
I had returned to the wild shore,
The same moon higher in the sky,
The same silvery pathway there
On the silent waves. But now
I saw a figure walk that road
Her feet were barely touching it.
Immortal, goddess, beautiful
As that same starry heaven.
I was afraid.

Her skin glistened with the moon's kiss,
White marble now, now translucent
As glass, her veins pulsing ichor,
Dark gold visible, all within.
Her hair coiled like folds of black cream,
Her eyes were darkness flecked with stars
And on her head the same bright horns
Held a circle both silver and gold
Alternating in the night.
My eyes dazzled.

From one pale shoulder hung a cloak
Of midnight blue spangled with stars
Of every constellation,
The radiance of a million years.
And in her white right hand she held
A rod of twisted gold which shook
With tiny shards of light and sang
To the waves in silvery sound.
And with this enchanting wand
She touched my mouth.

"Do you know me, poor mortal soul?"
Her voice was like the murmur of the
earth
That makes the firm ground tremble.
"For I am known by many names
Among the nations: Demeter
And Aphrodite, Queen of Heaven
And the Night, Lady of the Sun.
To some I am the warlike Kali,
To others the Great Mother.
But to you,

"I am Isis, Lady of the Two Lands,
Mistress of the dangerous seas,
Goddess of the life-warming Sun,
The bringer of life, protectress
Of those who wander in the shades.
I am all things, all divinities,
And I have come to you this night,
This long night, to bring you comfort.
On the edge of freezing death
I offer life."

Her voice, her golden sistrum
On my lips had struck me dumb,
My heart a desert night filled with myrrh.
She took me in her bloodless arms
And plunged by body in the sea,
Now an ocean of blood that filled
My breath and swelled my torpid veins,
As if a hundred thousand altars
Had yielded sacrifices
To the depths.

I cannot tell how long I lay
Or drifted on that scarlet sea.
But in the East the first bright rays
Of the rising Sun scalded with gold
The goddess's arms, her face, her breasts.
And I could feel the pulse of joy,
Pleasure beyond joy, beyond sex,
Beyond life itself pulse in me.
My blood flowed warmly again
And I lived.

"Sleep now, returned to life, to peace.
Forget the one you lost. He is
My special care among the souls
Of peaceful, gentle night. He rests.
And I will send another to you
Who will bring love into your veins
And fill your days with happiness.
And you will prosper in my love.
I have only one request:
Do not forget me."

How could I forget the mistress
Of my life, the one who bought me,
Dead in all but breath, with the Sun's
gold
And filled me with the elixir
Of love once more? Lady Isis,
I'll worship you and honour you
Until my last breath draws me down
To the sea of forgetfulness
Once more. You are my goddess,
My religion.

And I've kept my word. The immortal one
Remains in my soul. Months had passed
And peace was on my brow, my eyes
Shone with her own silvery light.
I'll not forget the man I lost,
He stays a part of me, the dark
Night-time of my unhappy soul.
But I'd live in the world again,
My mouth touched by the bright
Wand of life.

And so, the Sun hung low on other sands,
Not far from where I'd died that night.
A golden sun of blood and sea
That shone on your face like satin.
You smiled and we drank wine and talked
Until the evening star shone there
In the same heaven, and you crept
Cautiously into my heart. The warmth
Of you told me that Isis
Kept her promise.

THE
PROPHECY

PALIMPSEST

You are my hidden word, my palimpsest,
A page rewritten every day where true
Erasure leaves a faint, visible test
Of older happiness beneath the new.

And as with things we cherish in that
way,
When there is nothing left for me to write,
I must anticipate the mournful day
That language fails me. Sometimes in the
night

I'll linger by the doorway while you sleep
When all the house is dyed with
moonlight's brush
And, just to understand your breathing,
creep
Closer. Or in the early morning wash

Of Sun lying low upon your face –
Curled among the scribbled linen sheets –

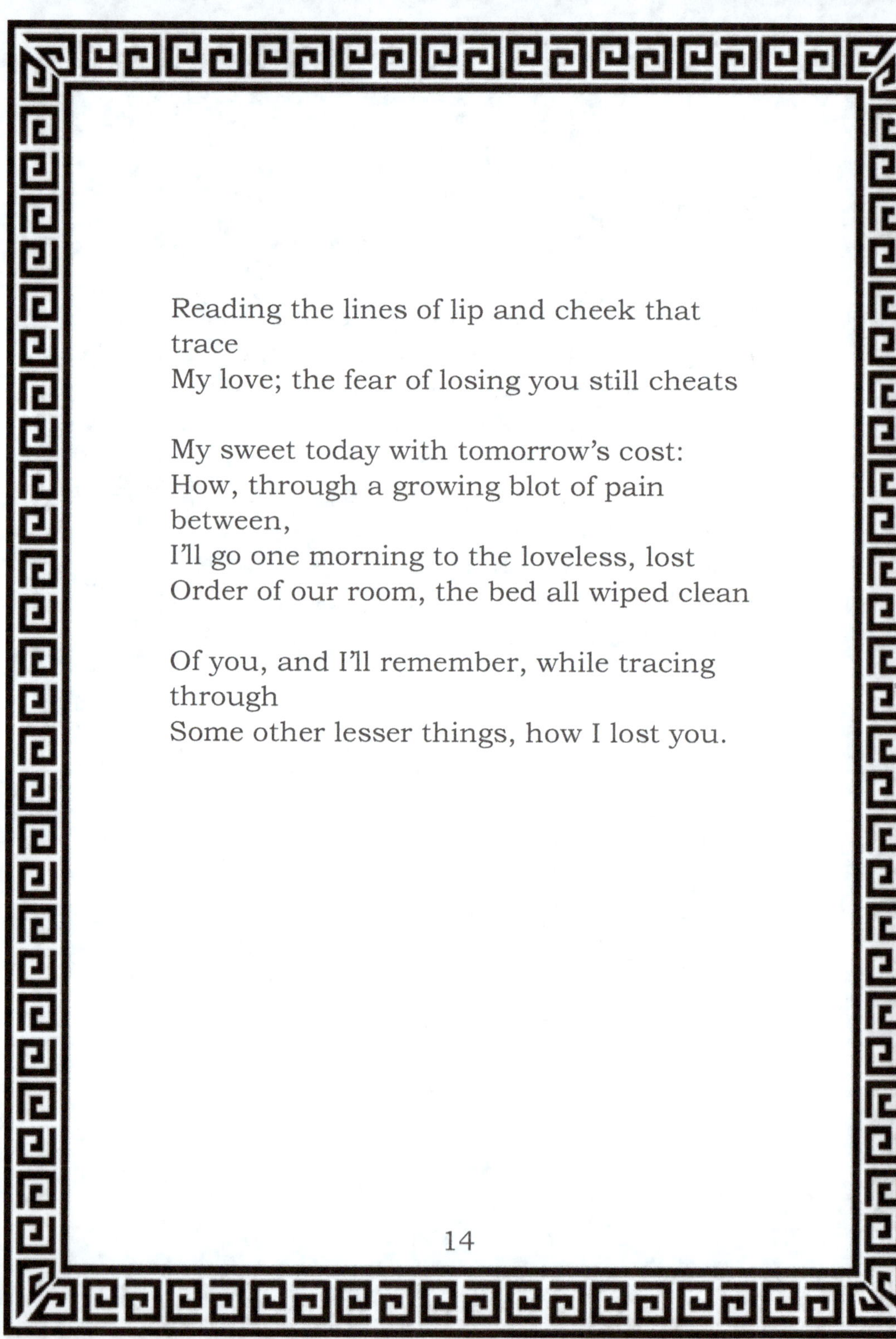

Reading the lines of lip and cheek that trace
My love; the fear of losing you still cheats

My sweet today with tomorrow's cost:
How, through a growing blot of pain between,
I'll go one morning to the loveless, lost
Order of our room, the bed all wiped clean

Of you, and I'll remember, while tracing through
Some other lesser things, how I lost you.

A CIGARETTE CASE

A night of cigarettes and drinks,
Small chatter with the Earls Court
sphynx:
She's off again! – Vada the bona eke
In late-night Soho bars mid-week,
Of subtle signs and indiscrete
Dodging of roughs on Carnaby Street.
A taxi back to a gift-wrapped box
From somewhere richly orthodox.
"I was worried we might lose it;
I should've let you choose it."
His sleepy "No" beyond the dutiful
Contemplating something beautiful:

I am the red-gold lines of twisted rope
Bevelled edges and a satisfying click,
And within my open shell an envelope
Of silver silk ribbon, I offer slick
Ranks of pardonably clean, white
cigarettes
Gold-capped and tight as new parade
cadets.

Pocket-sized precious, love sings
In gold. He'd never owned things
So fine.
          "And where did you get this?"
"He gave it me" – just one more kiss –
But all the while his cheeks redden deep
Under police lights; his eyes want sleep.
"He says you stole it?" He looks blank.
"Why would he, and I'll be quite frank,
A man like him give you a gift
Like this? Surely you must have lifted
It from his flat"; "He's a decent gent,
Upstanding, not like you, a pansy rent."

 "He said he loved me!" The heart in this
way
Breaks. A little weakness, a tight-lipped
fear,
Three times denied the secret passion
play
Of Earls Court. And the dull, tired Super's
sneer

Of intimation: "Yes, he'll make a trim
Confession if he knows what's good for
him."

Confess to what? To loving well,
But not wisely? To robbing Hell
For a little heaven?
                          A "How long
Ago? The Coleherne, an old song
Playing. You looked so young... I thought,
Barely legal." And then they'd fought
Over nothing, small jealousies,
The trust implied by a set of keys;

A case lifted from its plush place
Seals it, grateful fingers trace
A "thank you" in the moment wild bloods
roar.
And later a loud knocking on the door.

It wasn't done to love then without
shame,

The copper's stare, the "somehow things
don't fit";
And who amongst us wouldn't say the
same:
"I met him once, he must have stolen it."
Who wouldn't lie? – *mon semblable – mon
frère*
The lad's confession making all things
square.

MASSACRE OF THE INNOCENTS

Long ago mystic painters told
How peace would leave the earth in wild
Eyed prophetic colours, on the immense
fold
Of universal night: a holy child

Wrapped tight in his mother's shimmering
hem
Blue as heaven against the winter cold;
The flares of sentinels in Bethlehem
Branding passing faces with red and gold.

"Pass on," they say. "And though the
mountains shake
With thunder, pay no heed. Pass on once
more,
Though still the howling hungry jackals
slake
Their thirst for blood, towards that alien
shore

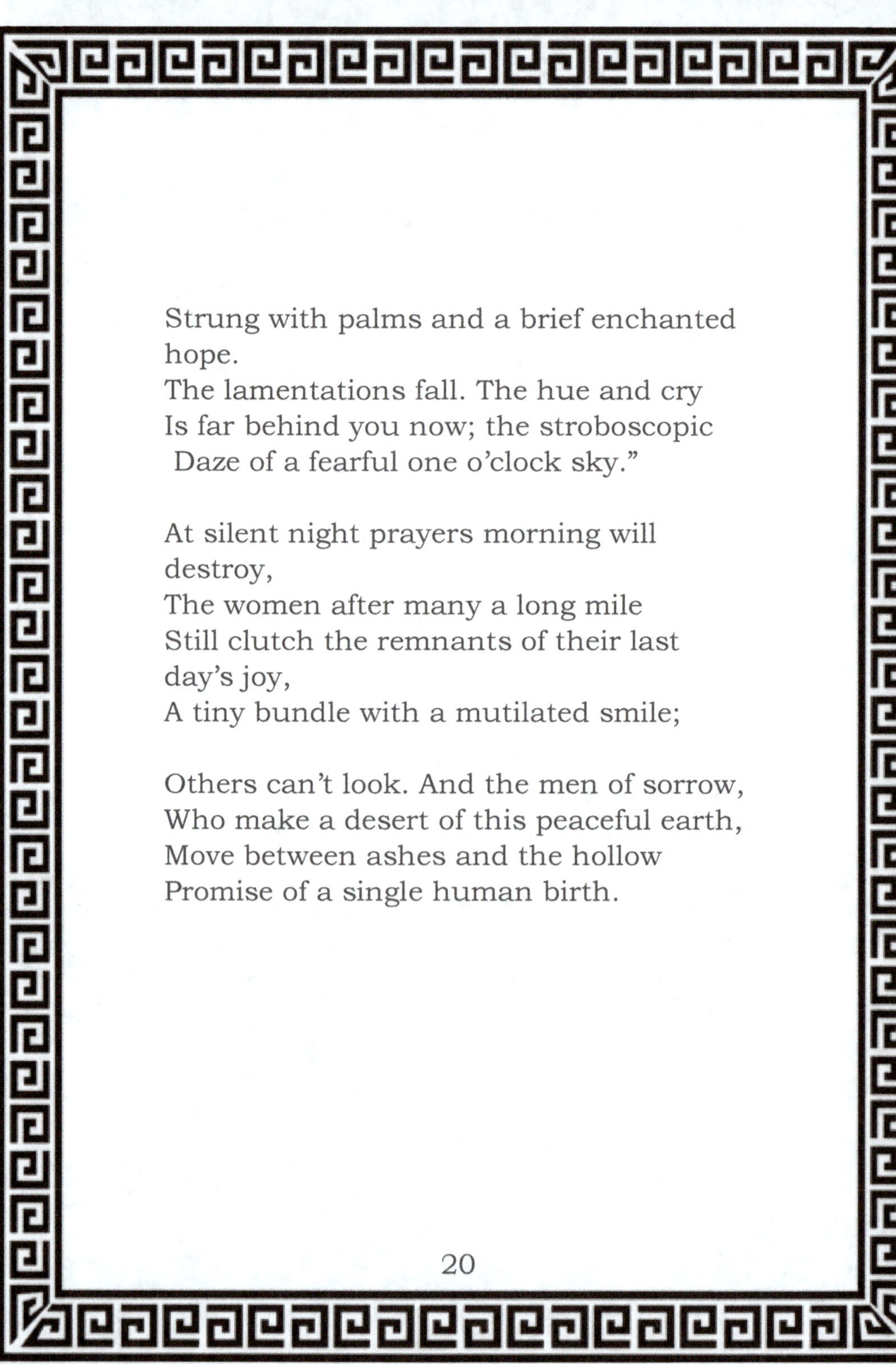

Strung with palms and a brief enchanted
hope.
The lamentations fall. The hue and cry
Is far behind you now; the stroboscopic
 Daze of a fearful one o'clock sky."

At silent night prayers morning will
destroy,
The women after many a long mile
Still clutch the remnants of their last
day's joy,
A tiny bundle with a mutilated smile;

Others can't look. And the men of sorrow,
Who make a desert of this peaceful earth,
Move between ashes and the hollow
Promise of a single human birth.

AFTER TINTORETTO, THE BRERA

Isn't it just that others draw a veil
On grief, while tears drop hot like Arabic
Upon your cheeks, and on your brow the
pale
Light falls as if dawn had broke, niobic,

On a winter's day – "He is not dead!"
The outstretched arms embracing air
Would dearly touch what they clearly
dread.
A sob parts dumb lips, a loose strand of
hair

Betrays the agony transfixing you.
"Be not afraid", you are the one chosen
Beyond the rest, though the once ample
dew
Of independent thought stands frozen,

Incomprehensible. Turn that sad gaze
On what's to come. A red desert morning,

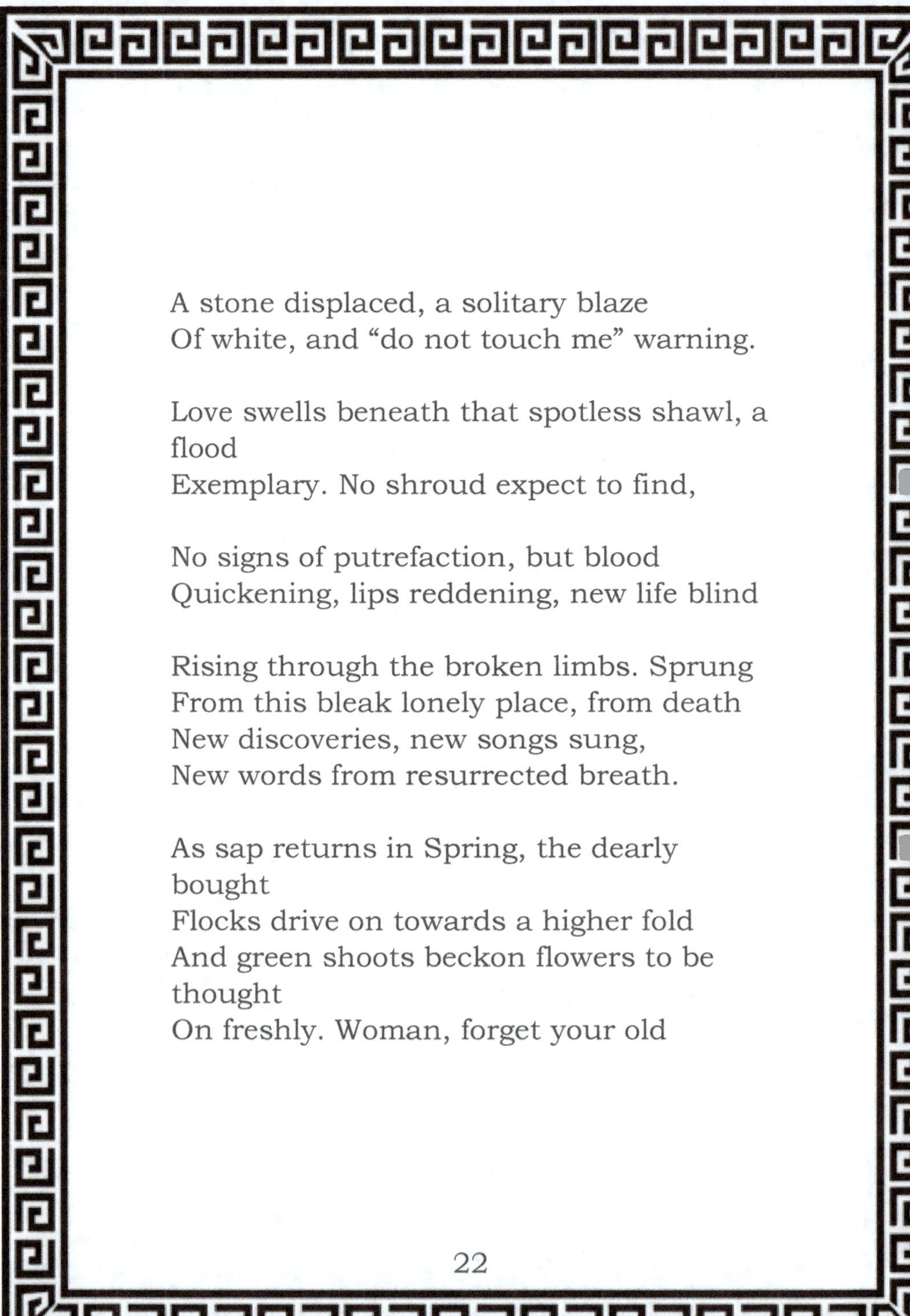

A stone displaced, a solitary blaze
Of white, and "do not touch me" warning.

Love swells beneath that spotless shawl, a
flood
Exemplary. No shroud expect to find,

No signs of putrefaction, but blood
Quickening, lips reddening, new life blind

Rising through the broken limbs. Sprung
From this bleak lonely place, from death
New discoveries, new songs sung,
New words from resurrected breath.

As sap returns in Spring, the dearly
bought
Flocks drive on towards a higher fold
And green shoots beckon flowers to be
thought
On freshly. Woman, forget your old

Bed of unhappy making, liberal
With the soul's winter – "Life everlasting
Still you will find" – and in the interval
Short as a winter's day, mourn love's
passing,

Let the darkness hold it like a bud
Buried in earth until new colours spill
Across drawn lineaments like flesh and
blood,
And give due credit to universal skill.

ISOLDE

In the wild Spring I'll stand on the shore
And listen to the never quiet sea.
Pebbles chatter like market day,
And mention with the waves your name;
Your body's remembrance on the salt
spray.

I walk through decorated meadows
Beyond the castle wall, my women
Waiting patient for me to turn,
But the breeze would whisper, and I linger
Longing to hear some news of you.

Even the brook that cools my feet
Will not resolve me, each thing I see,
Hear or touch reminds my heart
That necessary smiles profane
The absence of its true lord.

And through the dark suggestive night,
The bed I loathe for not being yours
Detains me, yet before my eyes,
Shut in by sleep, you materialise
As clear as surf, brook and air.

BONFIRE NIGHT

We spoke last night, the moon and I,
    As an early frost was forming
And the crack and fizz of the dropping sky
    Had settled to quiet morning.

I asked her when my love returns,
    So long and far away;
How the heart yearns and the body burns
    To fill up the delay

With every act and every sense
    Invariably foreseen –
A vacant room, a dull pretence
    Of living in between.

"But wait a while," the moon replied,
    "I've seen your love, I know it –
For whatever midnight's shadows hide
    I've light enough to show it."

She frowned, as an awkward little cloud
    Had settled on her cheek.

An earnest moon, she was too proud
    For playing hide-and-seek.

It passed; she thought a long, long while:
    "I know that it was he –
He had a very fetching smile
    For everyone, you see.

"He laughed and danced and drank his fill
    Till the stars made a shining wreath,
Then he lay on his bed so very still
    I could hardly see him breathe."

"Send him a kiss," I ventured to smile,
    Though my heart was sorely hot,
For fear had made a ready trial
    Of things I know not what.

"A kiss?" she asked. "One kiss? All right!
    The least he deserves, I'd say,
Though the angels kiss his head tonight
    And he sleeps through breaking day."

I thanked her but to one who passed
    The scene was nothing strange.
Though we spoke, no words came thick or
fast.
    The moon's face didn't change.

No lover wept with drooping eye
    At an empty windowsill.
Just a man stood shivering at the sky
    In a sudden morning chill.

WAR SONG

Yes, it's true, I loved that Sherwood lad.
You always knew it would be one like him:
At nineteen a corporal, cap this side of
mad.
Peace would have rated our chances slim
For love, but he was innocent of sad
Charades – his life was still a school day
hymn –
And in the thud, bloody thud, rat-a-tat
making
War, he'd hold me tightly to stop me
shaking.

And yes, I should have known the
wretched end
Was not enough to be a Sunday hero,
When the sly Colonel's quick to
apprehend:
"They censor letters from the front, you
know."
Twixt shame and death, death was my
true friend,

No man's land a convenient road show
By which this inconvenient warrior's head
Was crowned with wire and painted
honourable red.

Forgive me, dearest, for the brave young
men
Whose love and love of war have brought
you sorrow.
Forgive me for what can never be again,
But where I lie, we disregard tomorrow:
Snow falls in the vacancy, all ken
Of time lost. Lakes and rivers borrow
Blue from blue and sigh 'qui tacet
consentire'.
Where Alpine roots twine, binding me to
soft clay,

Years back it was, you found me, kissed
my name,
Stone and earth a meagre barricade;
And were it given me so to frame,

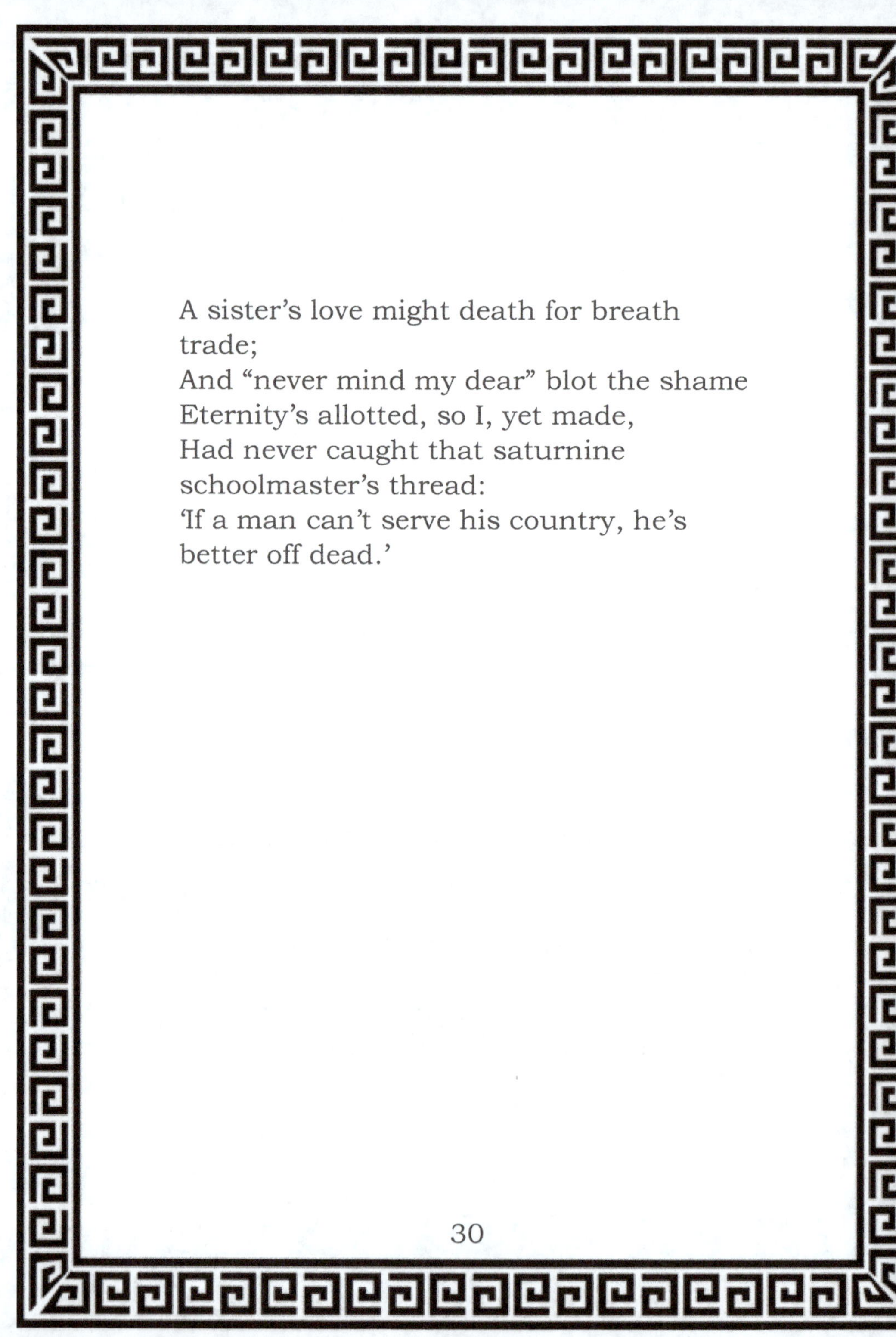

A sister's love might death for breath
trade;
And "never mind my dear" blot the shame
Eternity's allotted, so I, yet made,
Had never caught that saturnine
schoolmaster's thread:
'If a man can't serve his country, he's
better off dead.'

THE TELESCOPE (FOR MY FATHER)

I see you standing in the line of fire,
Faithful, far off in place and time,
An evening when the insect choir
Should murmur peace. Instead sublime

War annihilates the hours beside.
As if through a telescopic eye
Distant figures become magnified,
In a red-hot dance twist and leap and fly.

A little closer, a new cosmos yields
New ranks tending a new mission
Of black-board equations, magnetic fields,
Or new strategies of atomic fission:

A material metaphysician
Reconciling particles to God
With the wisdom of the great magician
Who drew down Spheres to dance about
his rod.

Closer, and the brain world merges
shapes
Of sea and sky, your brush now tracing
lines
Which chalk and fire once drew; glowing
landscapes,
Shutter-sharp pencil strokes of vines and
shrines.

Closer still, and soldier, teacher, painter
blur.
I'm left with shadows: bright talk,
debonair,
The past, memory on the sharp spur
Of tears, rosaries, words, an empty chair.

BROKEN

Michelangelo strolling by
The old Signoria, thoughts
On the town's defences,
Did he stop to contemplate
Why David had a broken arm?
Did he mind his work was fractured
Or wonder how the fragments
Had been spirited away?
Perhaps he simply shrugged,
Continued his not untroubled path
To the Soprintendenza's door –
A report to make,
A reputation to defend.
Was it all unfinished business,
Broken pieces, failed designs,
A simple case of artist's block? Unless
Some higher-purposed good stood by
Dictating preferential details,
Beyond the meaning of broken stone,
The mutilated image of a man,
For the common book of history.

DIXIE CEMETERY

It seemed to be basking
One wing outstretched, only
The rapid palpitation
Of its body, the eye
Shiny and black, staring
And the smear of red on the grass.
Nearby a bright green iguana
More than a foot long
Lurched behind a gravestone
To wait our moving on.
There was no hurry
The bird was going nowhere,
But the hot afternoon
Suggesting violent death
Stopped us in our tracks.

A NEW YEAR

Not drink! When all the world's
prescribing
Cocktails of an old malt rain,
The earth is sodden from imbibing
And doesn't favour grape from grain.

The very elements are drowned
In pink gin sunsets on the beach
And black velvet night has crowned
The mountain tops' snowball reach.

The Sun's so far gone in his cup
He hasn't shown his face since noon,
Having kept his sister up
On sundowners amber moon,

He'd rather sleep the old year off
In clouds of burning whisky mist
And suck the tap and swill the quaff
Until the heavens drop down pissed.

The birds are singing in the trees
But not for love of melody;

They've all got tipsy on sea breeze
And sling not sing their threnody.

Stags stagger, eagles reel, jugged
Hares box and ginger cheer's foxed the
fox.
Old brown beer burns foam unplugged
And fish sip Scotch lochs on the rocks.

Sobriety's not nature's way
When bad and mad are all the trend.
Cold dawn, no matter how grey
Looks better through a bottle's end.

So let's forget this mouldy year
Of trumps and shocks and folktales grim,
Let's raise a bubbling glass frontier
To drink the New in on its brim.

Drink the New and drink the Old,
Mothers, fathers, gone between.
Lovers who have left the fold,
And drink no more the evergreen!

BARBARIANS

And mountains live in senses, so they
say,
A chill pricking of the skin on a summer's
day
A shadow on the earth, a feeling
Of secret colour subtly stealing
Upon a steel-blue edge in distant light
Now turning amethyst on closer sight.

Mountains are anomalies, a fold
In the earth, grey streaked with fool's
gold;
A torrent of rock in steep reverse
Defying gravity's ancient curse;
A swell of bodies where one strains
Beneath the other, tracing the remains,
The hollows of some strong-fingered god
Frenzied by the joy of rank and rod-
Fierce passion.
          Old men raised with pride
For ancient murders here stand petrified,

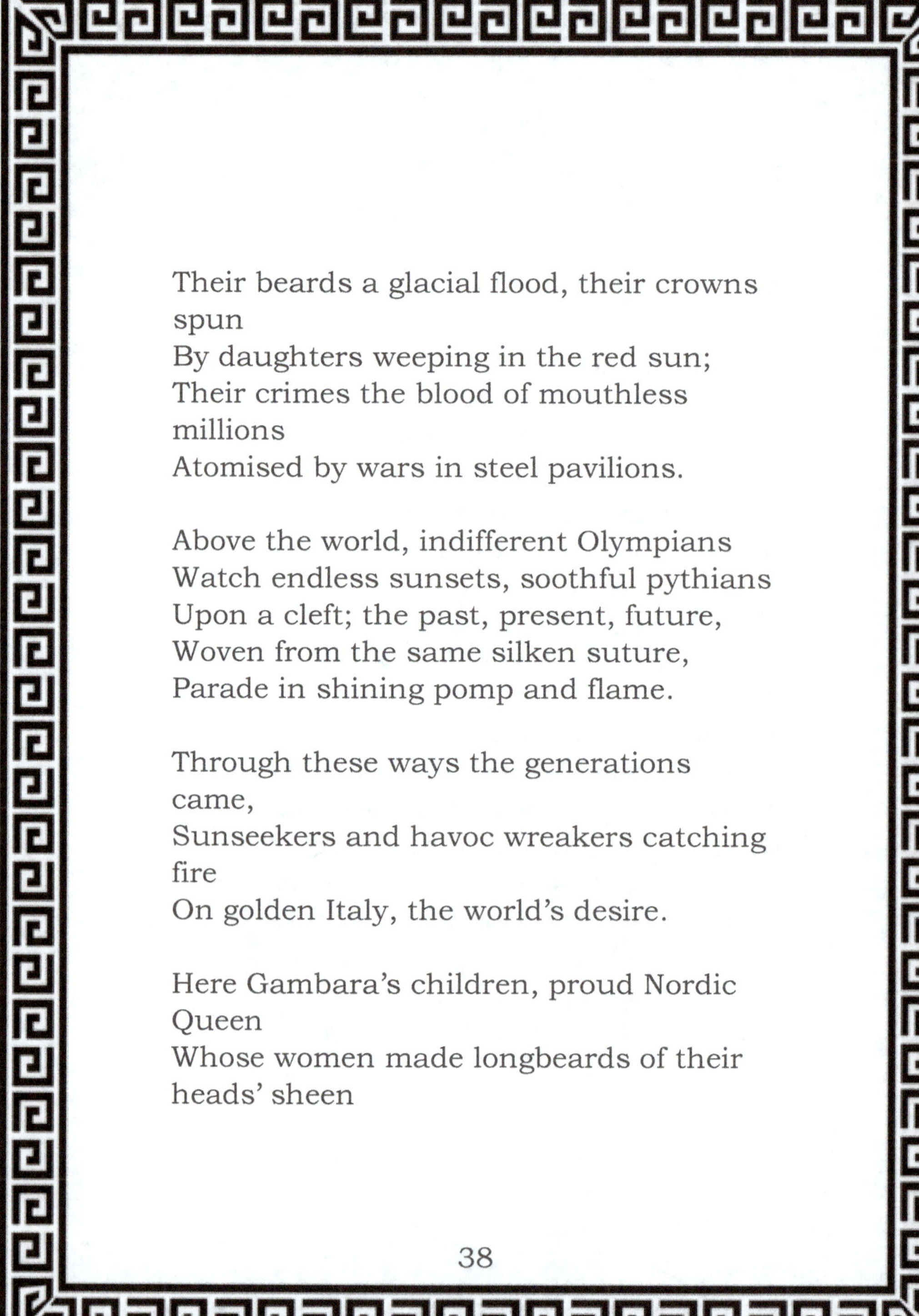

Their beards a glacial flood, their crowns
spun
By daughters weeping in the red sun;
Their crimes the blood of mouthless
millions
Atomised by wars in steel pavilions.

Above the world, indifferent Olympians
Watch endless sunsets, soothful pythians
Upon a cleft; the past, present, future,
Woven from the same silken suture,
Parade in shining pomp and flame.

Through these ways the generations
came,
Sunseekers and havoc wreakers catching
fire
On golden Italy, the world's desire.

Here Gambara's children, proud Nordic
Queen
Whose women made longbeards of their
heads' sheen

That with her sons, through Freya's
cunning fraud,
Victory might be shared without the
sword,
They followed the rivers and peaks in
silent awe
Of a new-found homeland; the first who
saw
The glittering plain that's born their name
Across the centuries of fault and fame.

And these split mountain tops of rock and
rime
Inspired the soul of Goethe with Sublime
Restless thoughts. The scholar poet given
From northern mist to sun streaming in
heaven,
Filling those empty names he'd read in
books
With flesh and pulse and gentle passing
looks,
So he might ask beneath another moon,
"Kennst du das Land wo die Zitronen
Blühn?"

We are all pilgrims on the mountain top
The promised land beneath us, yet we
stop
And linger in the world of rock and sky
Pleased to be nearer heaven's clearer eye,
Wary of the weary trek before us,
The long descent to peoples who ignore
us;
Whose perfect lives (or so we think) go on

Oblivious to our wild barbarian song.
Soon we'll be on our way. Before we die
We'll not pass by their gates. We'll sit and
sigh
Beside the violet sea, and listen to
The Siren's voice within the hullabaloo
Of civilising waves that crash and fall
But never steal us from the old mead hall,
The bardic harp and runes of memory,
However sweet that warm imagined Italy.

Soon, but first between bright flowers and
ebbing snow
We'll sit and wonder where those hours of
pleasure go.

FIVE SONNETS (AFTER MICHELANGELO)

I

Here at last, my fucking Odyssey,
Tempest-tossed, in a leaky boat, is come
To that common port, to pay the nightly
sum,
As all must do, of our mortality.

I see now fantasy's extreme
Dream made of love an idol, not a tool,
Bound in shackles, like some stupid fool,
To the headlong rush of his careering
team.

What use was breathing in the open air,
Sweating sex and drugs, if double harms
Are waiting for me: death and mortal fear

Of it? Nothing I've done can now compare
To that proud deity who opened up her
arms
Wide across the universe to draw me
near.

II

Whose knife, flickering little soul,
Peels away your tired old hide?
When will cruel Time decide
To set you free and make you whole?

I might change my skin in these last, few
years
But I can't change my sin with burning
tears.
I won't pretend I don't envy the dead,
Nor long for an end to this soulless dread.

Love, in my final hours,
Turn from your Thrones and Powers,
Burn those topless towers

Of pride from which ambition flew.
Reach out to me, merciful and true,
Strip me from myself and make me new.

III

And I don't know if it's the natal light
Of whichever god made it my soul feels,
Or if some great love I once knew peels
Back the slough of memory to shine
bright

Again, or if the shadows of sleep
That has long evaded me now lace
My sight with I know not what burning
trace,
And this, perhaps, is what makes tears
seep

From my eyes. For now, when I walk, he
who
Guides me is not with me; nor can I see
Where he's gone, I'm blind to
circumstance.

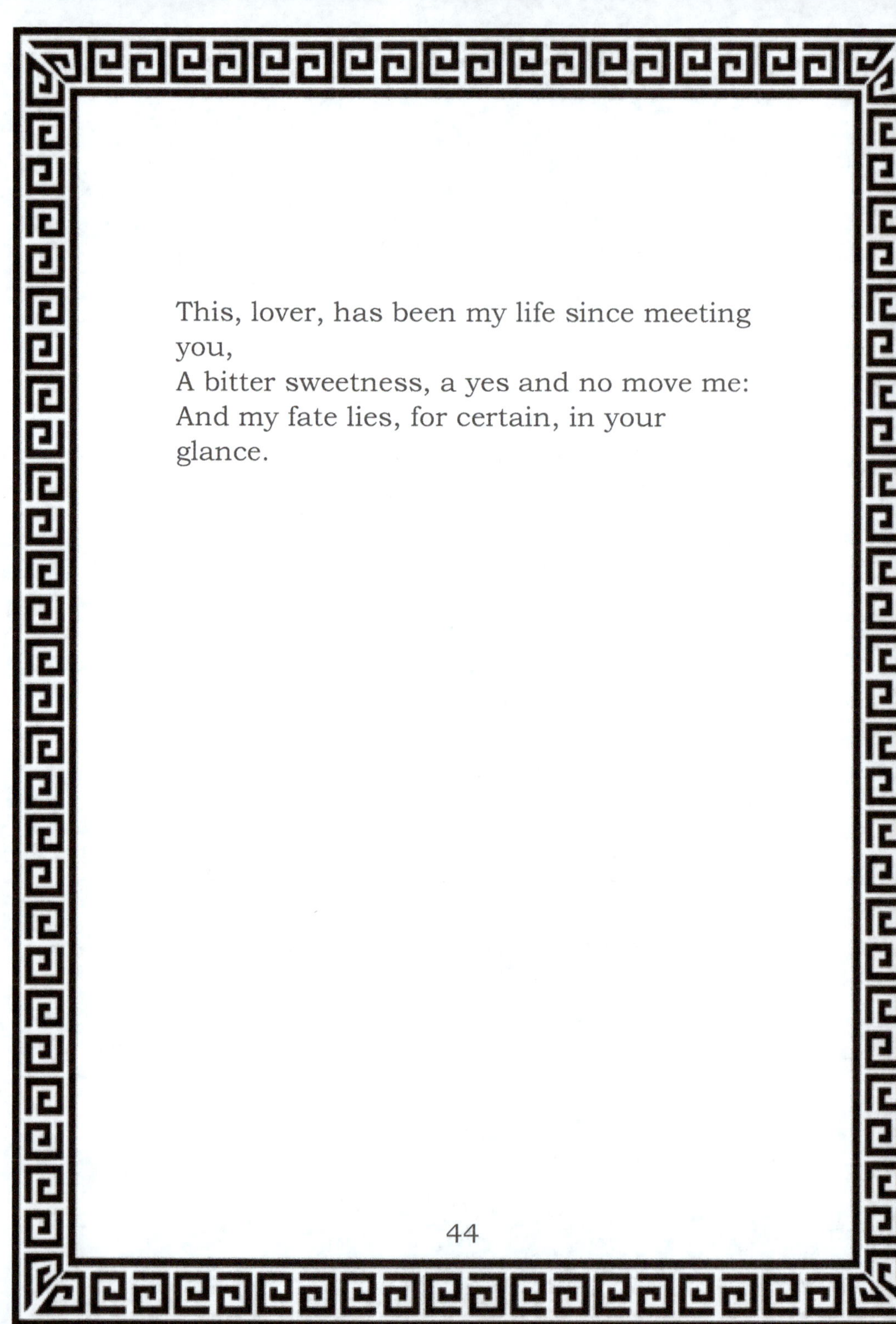

This, lover, has been my life since meeting
you,
A bitter sweetness, a yes and no move me:
And my fate lies, for certain, in your
glance.

IV

Now everything is holy in my eyes
And beauty is the end-all of my soul.
My heart throbs in the sacramental ties
Of passion, and love must take its toll.

Particulars don't matter, I am dumb
With longing, a sweet, narcotic chain
Binds me fast, so I must still succumb
To desire's exquisite fucking pain.

And yet if he can temper me and blend
Body and soul, each to each belonging,
The heat of fusion might put an end
To every purely human longing.

But I am lead, my veins will never glow
With gold, I am a humble manakin,
A target for the fiery boy whose bow
Has made a rag tag of this tattered skin.

V

If one desire, if one great sympathy,
If one future governs two lovers,
If one's misfortune lays low the other's,
If one spirit two hearts can oversee;

If one soul in two bodies ever-lasts,
Consensual ecstasy on equal wings;
If Love's indifferent hand bends and
strings
His golden bow to fuse our binary hearts;

If one loves the other and neither himself,
With every sinew joined, then one shot
Will tie into a single pulse our blood:

A thousand futures intervene, their
wealth
A hundred times falls short of such a
knot;
And so we stand the ebbing of the flood.

BREATHE

Where the waters move like steel, brushed
Under a white sky, the world breathes;
Where grey pebbles rub the soles
Of our feet and dead leaves greave
In pockets on the shore;

Where the forest darkens the earth
With green and moss and fallen trunks,
Bright fungi lighting the way,
Horse, Orange Peel, Fly Agaric, Deathcap,
Like a paintbox spilled out of time.

Breath flies out into the cool, still air
And nothing but the sound of footfall
Troubles the old, old silence.
Where you were the moss and earth
Took on your body's imprint.

"Breathe, won't you. Just breathe for me."
You fell like an oak, a few paces ahead,
Lying there a moment, cradled by dead
leaves

And soft pine needles, my palms
pounding
Your cool heart – "just breathe damn
you!" –

And the sick milk of panic polluting my
veins.

All I could think to do was sing.
I held your head as the words came
Choking from my throat. Heavy and
heavier
My burden, colder than the waters of the
loch
And deeper than my sorrow.

"Breathe" for the rain is falling softly now
And a crowd of midges settles – "breathe"
And we will start again, do things
differently.
Just stay with me on the earth, this
beautiful earth,
And I'll wipe clean your mouth of spit.

Your head is heavy like a purple rock,
Your lungs only rise when I press my
mouth
To yours. Your hand's like marble.

"Will I die today?" you'd asked a hundred
times
When wine made sleep crack open like
A paper cut in your head – "You won't, I
promise."
"Will I die today?" you'd asked that very
morning
And I'd given you my usual reply.

The dog's running in the woods now,
scared,
Or was that years ago. Time has become a
stone.
The calls of rescue when there was none.
How long has it been? An hour, a day, a
life?
The moss grows between my toes and the
damp

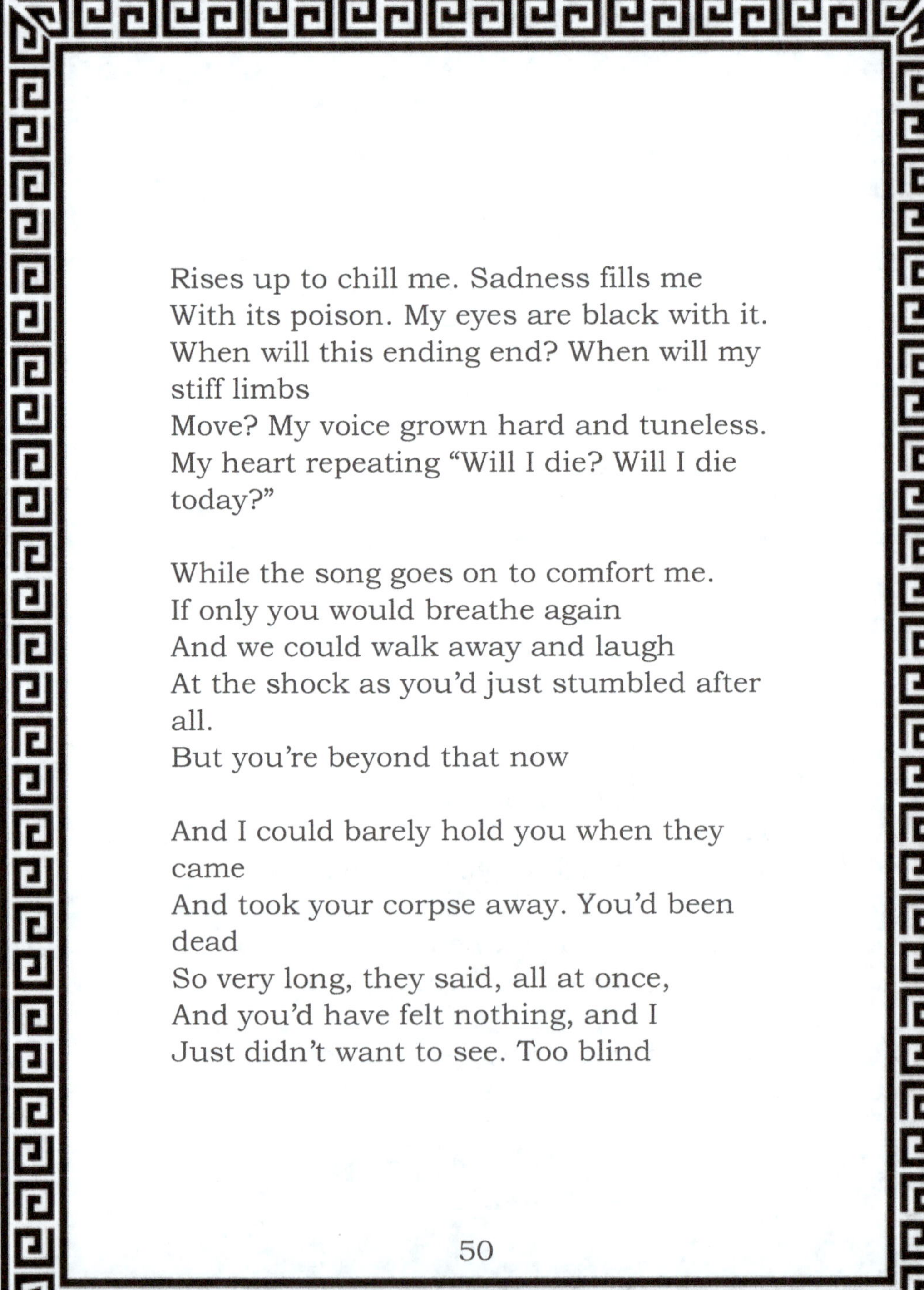

Rises up to chill me. Sadness fills me
With its poison. My eyes are black with it.
When will this ending end? When will my
stiff limbs
Move? My voice grown hard and tuneless.
My heart repeating "Will I die? Will I die
today?"

While the song goes on to comfort me.
If only you would breathe again
And we could walk away and laugh
At the shock as you'd just stumbled after
all.
But you're beyond that now

And I could barely hold you when they
came
And took your corpse away. You'd been
dead
So very long, they said, all at once,
And you'd have felt nothing, and I
Just didn't want to see. Too blind

With tears to say goodbye. It seemed
Unfathomable. Your body flying in the air
While your spirit lingered on the earth.
And I knew I would never see you, here or
there,
Unless the gods are true or death a curse.

Death is nothing to the dead but
everything
To the living. Every fear, every pain,
Every broken heart, and we are sleepless
Because of death. We pause and wonder
why
We entered a room or took the car keys

Or why we're even bothering to eat.
Your dead face is everywhere. It's
banished
The living image of your smile or sad-eyed
stare.
Your voice is only on recordings now,
And only misremembered in my head.

The sun came through and made the
waters
Of the loch shine like silver. It glinted
On raindrops falling from trees
And caught the helicopter's blades
That carried you into the sky, for a
moment.

And I stood in a landscape full of water,
Rain and tears and the lapping of the
waves.
It seemed a million years before you came,
A million more since you've been gone,
And I still stand in that dark and silent
wood.

My body is full of dark liquid, coagulated.
Moss and peat cover me over and roots
Dig into my soft flesh. My breathing
Is the breathing of the earth, heavy
With moisture and crawling things.
"Will I die today?" Little by little,
With every breath and every moment
Of our lives, we are all dying every day.

IN THE EARTH

THE DEATH OF PETRONIUS

*"… to the blasé emperor nothing was
smart and elegant unless Petronius had
given it his approval" Tacitus 'Annals'*

My sense of taste seems to dissolve
Along with all the rest, like candy
On the tongue – and I can savour
Nothing else. The amber wine
In silver cups (gold's too trashy)
And of those rich delicious things
Between us – rare comestibles –
I could make an inventory:
Of plover's eggs and dormice dipped
In honey, or a suckling pig
That flew here on its truffled wings;
chestnuts stuffed with figs and spice;
oyster stew, an elegantly cut
Moray; but what would be the point?
When every dish to me is unseasoned.

I drift and drift and drift… again
Perhaps it was the precious glass

That fell and shattered, better that
Than leave it to his flatterers – yet
It troubles me; and rose on rose,
Flowers I never thought becoming
Of a fool, their cloying scent
So necessary to me now,
Are swelling lurid at my wrists;
Even the music on this night
Cannot break my heart; perhaps
It's just the losing of it all.

The rhythm of a life ill spent
Can't justify the name of song,
Each note is doubtful – there was a time
I fancied myself a connoisseur
Of killing things; and beauty was
My lord, my sensual emperor;
The gem I wore about my thumb.
Each faculty was diamond sharp.
Beauty purchased, I know, like love
Has limits, frontiers of ennui
That circumscribe possession still.

And at this moment I can say
I have loved many, but none in truth,
I've treasured beauty, but let it go
Without a qualm, long I've worshipped
Indolence, though inaction
Hasn't saved me from the knife;
A well-placed word's enough to bring
It all about me as a storm
At sea ruins a young man's wealth.
And but for my failing sense,
My final will would be to laugh,
Scandalise their maudlin faces
With some light and racy verses
From that silver-tongued lad of mine.

Drink to me friends, I cannot leave
Life sober. I might regret the breach
Or think to mend it with some piece
Of abject flattery unheard
Of even such a one as I.
I have taught the lamps to make
A mockery of day: I've faced

The Asiatic foe at dice.
I have even bought a province
With the wealth of its own people;
I was a Roman once.

                    Surgeon!
Bind up my wrists, I'm not yet done.

There is a poem still to write,
A costly object to acquire,
A boy to love. I will flatter
Just to do all these once more.
I'll praise inconsequential lines:
The voice of no particular merit,
The mincing, perfumed songster's dance;
Perhaps it is enough to sing
The heartless beauty of the she
He calls his wife; enough to live.

But where's the pleasure in such things?

And why prolong the residue

Of what was never living? Stop!

There's little left. A broken cup,
A smattering of friends, enough
To fill a modest dining room.
A faculty for memory –
The names and dates, salacious crimes
Against true sensibility –
I've witnessed every sly debauch
And these shall be my testament.

The wine may have no taste, at least
It is not bitter and behold!
How rich the rose bowl water flows!
It is warm, it is warm.
Bring the fire close enough,
Let it burn my cheek so I
May seem to counterfeit true passion.

My pulse is languid, and I hear
Nothing but the rush of heaven.
Has my boy stopped? His looks

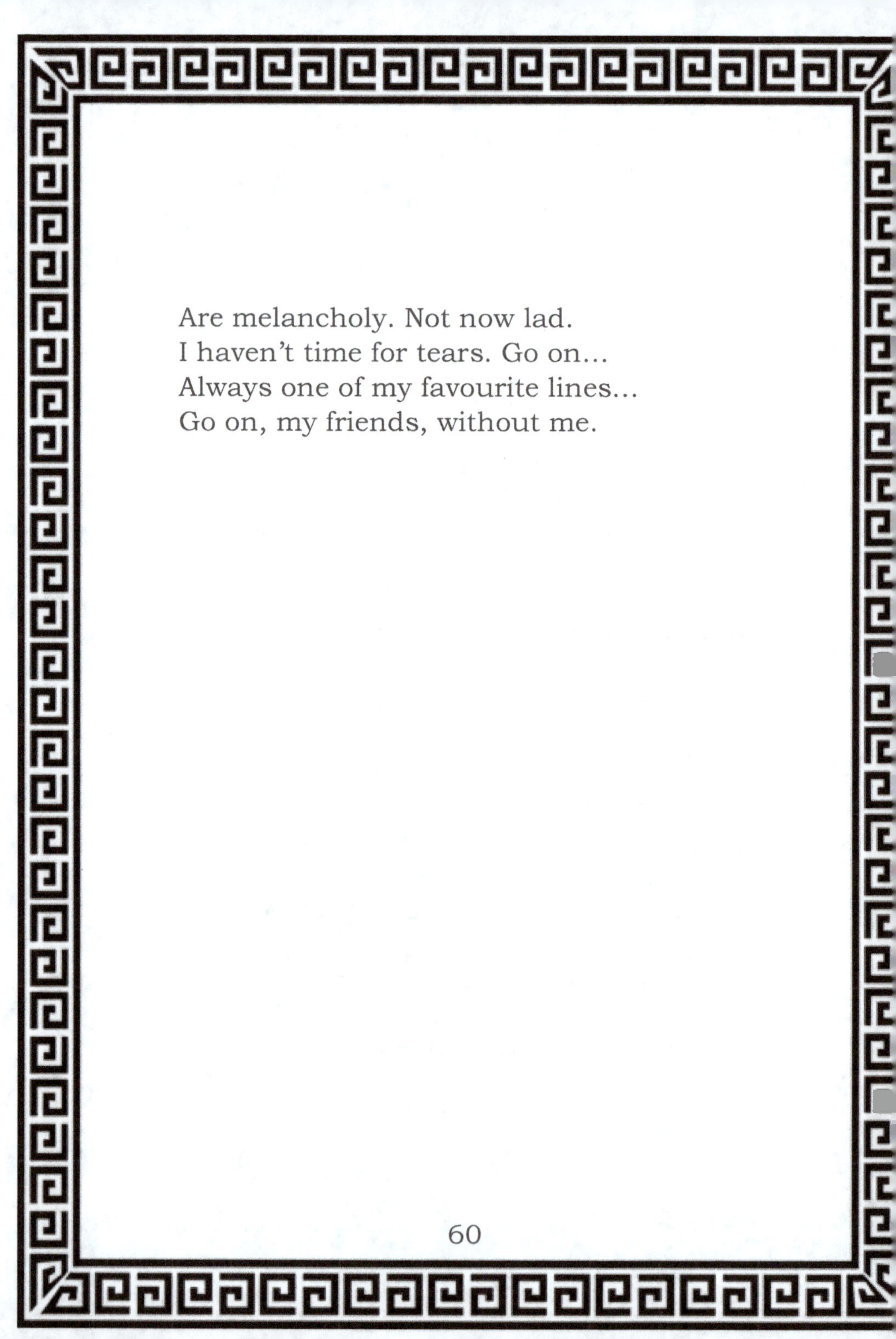

Are melancholy. Not now lad.
I haven't time for tears. Go on...
Always one of my favourite lines...
Go on, my friends, without me.

MER

I'd like to live beneath the sea
Where you are, and prick my soul
On coral and spiny creatures

Where you are, and not bleed,
I'd like to be where you are;
It's always cool amongst the kelp

And quiet from that long way
Down, where you are.
I'd like to smile at angel fish

And stroke the bellies of dolphins
From below, and be an atom
Of the great Ocean's glow,

A particle of the immense,
The diversity of living things
That is where you are,

Returning, like a drop of rain
Falling on the sea.
I'd like to feel my limbs twined

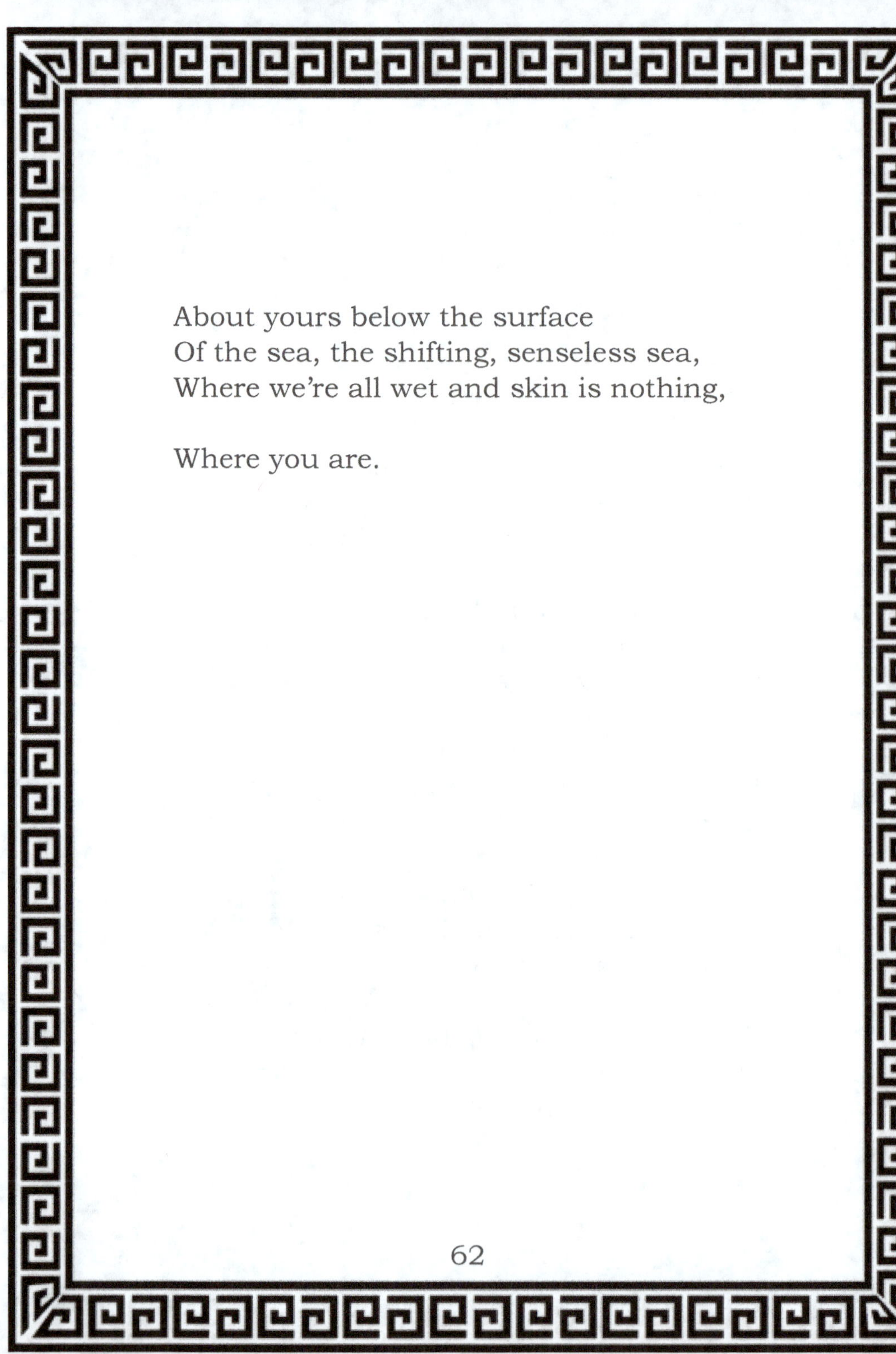

About yours below the surface
Of the sea, the shifting, senseless sea,
Where we're all wet and skin is nothing,

Where you are.

DYING EVERY DAY

We're dying every day they say.
The black ink of it is seeping
Slowly in our veins. The play
Of every moment is a moment
Nearer death.
And death is no beginning.

We're dying every day, so pause
And live a little with a little love.
Love is like a drug that takes us away
From all that dying.
It fills the night with day
An antidote to all that lying.

So, shoot me up a little love,
Let me feel it drive the dark away.
Shoot me up and fill the groove
Of me with love.

Love is like a drug, a potion
Of colours in the grey.
It keeps the dying every day away.

It's narcotic in the blood,
Adrenaline in the heart,
When death is no beginning.

So, shoot me up a little love,
Let me feel it drive the dark away.
Shoot me up and fill the groove
Of me with love.

And when the night is warm with it
And my body's full of it,
I will sink into your arms
And fuck away the dying every day.

So, shoot me up a little love,
Let me feel it drive the dark away.
Shoot me up and fill the groove
Of me with love.

CHTHONIC DIONYSUS (AFTER EURIPEDES)

I am Dionysus, son of Zeus
Born of woman in the forge of god's
Brilliant rage; man-god,
God of joy, man of sorrows.
Beside the troubled streams of Dirce
I came to the city of my birth,
No home or comfort, strangers here
Not kin, to punish and purify.
The one who comes to the threshold
With vines and figs and blood.
From the East, the lands of spice
Come my comrades, my wild ones,
To drive men mad with easy pleasure,
Stamping their feet to the beating drum
Filling the woods with their chanting
hymn;
Across the welcome mountainside
Sunk down at last upon the ground
After the dance, the holy fawn skin
Stretches red over their limbs.
With milk the earth flows,

Wine stains the meadows,
Honey from the bees
Pours out upon the rocks,
Torches blaze over the hillside,
The cry is up, the hunt is on
And won't be done till blood is drawn.
"When will we dance?" the maenads cry,
Leaping barefoot through the night
Heads flung back in ecstasy.
Taste the clear, cold dew on the air –
Like a fawn, a young doe
Springing high across the meadows –
Joyful to escape the hunt,
Like a storm-fed mountain stream,
Rejoicing in the level plain,
Amid the green wilderness.
Evoë Bacchoi! Evoë Bacchoi!
Celebrate the god of joy.

I NO LONGER KNOW MYSELF
(AFTER RUMI)

I no longer know myself.
Not Christian nor Jew, not Muslim nor
one
Who has no faith. I am not of the East
Nor of the West. I am from
No land, nor have I travelled any sea.
Outside of Nature, the stars have no claim
on me.
The sky's not my element. I am not of
the dust.

I have not lived in the world,
Nor will I in the next. I am no child
Of Adam or Eve or any myth of long
beginnings.
Neither male nor female, my name
Takes up no space, my flesh no bone.
I possess neither body nor soul.

I am his, his alone.

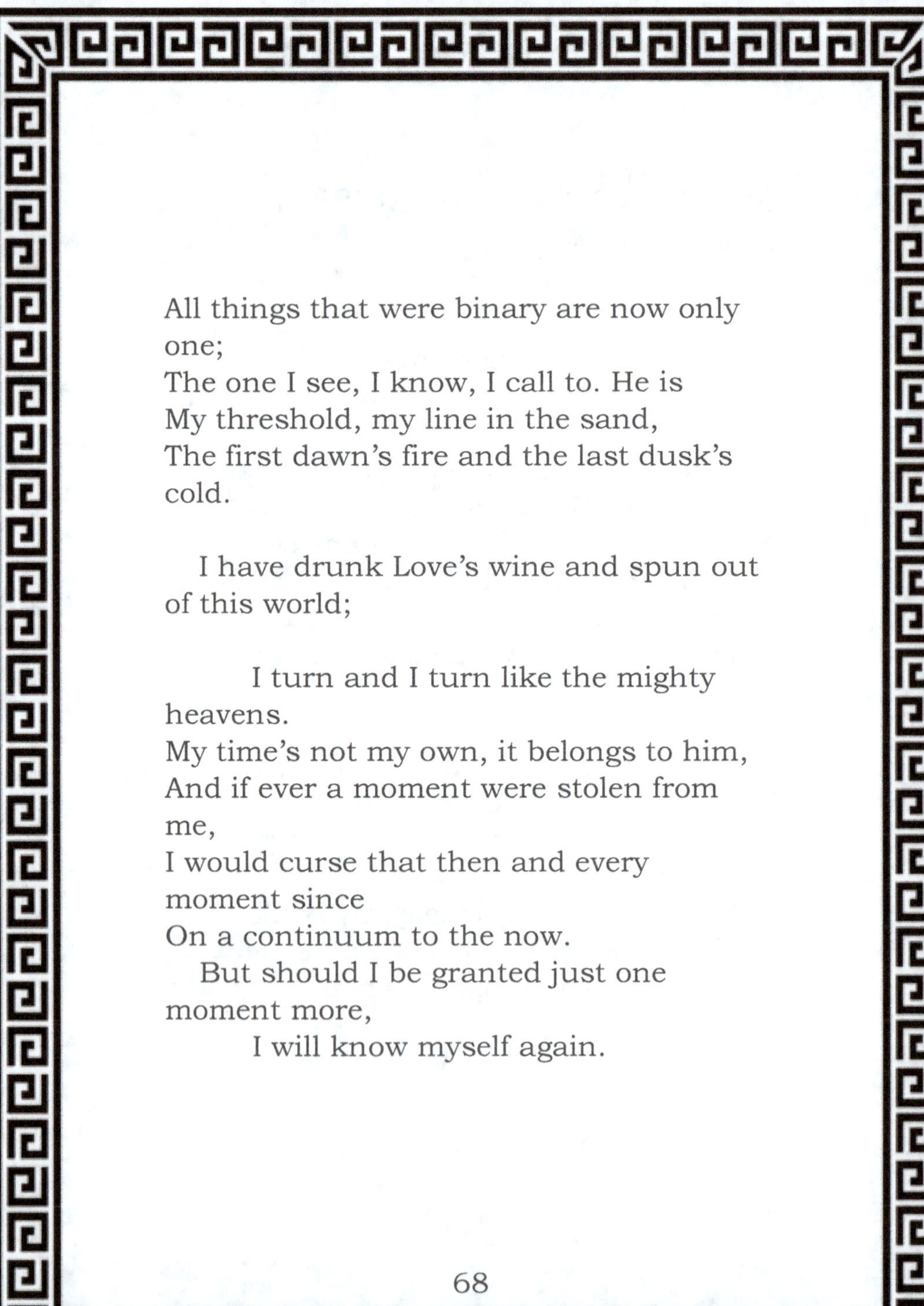

All things that were binary are now only
one;
The one I see, I know, I call to. He is
My threshold, my line in the sand,
The first dawn's fire and the last dusk's
cold.

   I have drunk Love's wine and spun out
of this world;

      I turn and I turn like the mighty
heavens.
My time's not my own, it belongs to him,
And if ever a moment were stolen from
me,
I would curse that then and every
moment since
On a continuum to the now.
   But should I be granted just one
moment more,
      I will know myself again.

WINTER SOLSTICE

And I was travelling a snowy track
The Sun, fallen from the zodiac,
Had struck the near horizon; clouds
Hung together in bloodied shrouds,

And on the last of this short day
Winter shot pearl on white and grey.
Fields stuck with shards of grass
Plunged to where the looking glass

Air held the movement of water
Within an iron hard halter.
But as the day, with all its right
Of silver, yielded to the night,

A red heat fused the Sun and tide
Like the petals of a rose blown wide;
As though the world's relentless climb
Reverted to a time before time,

Bare, brittle, beautiful,
A fresh start, a gentle lull,

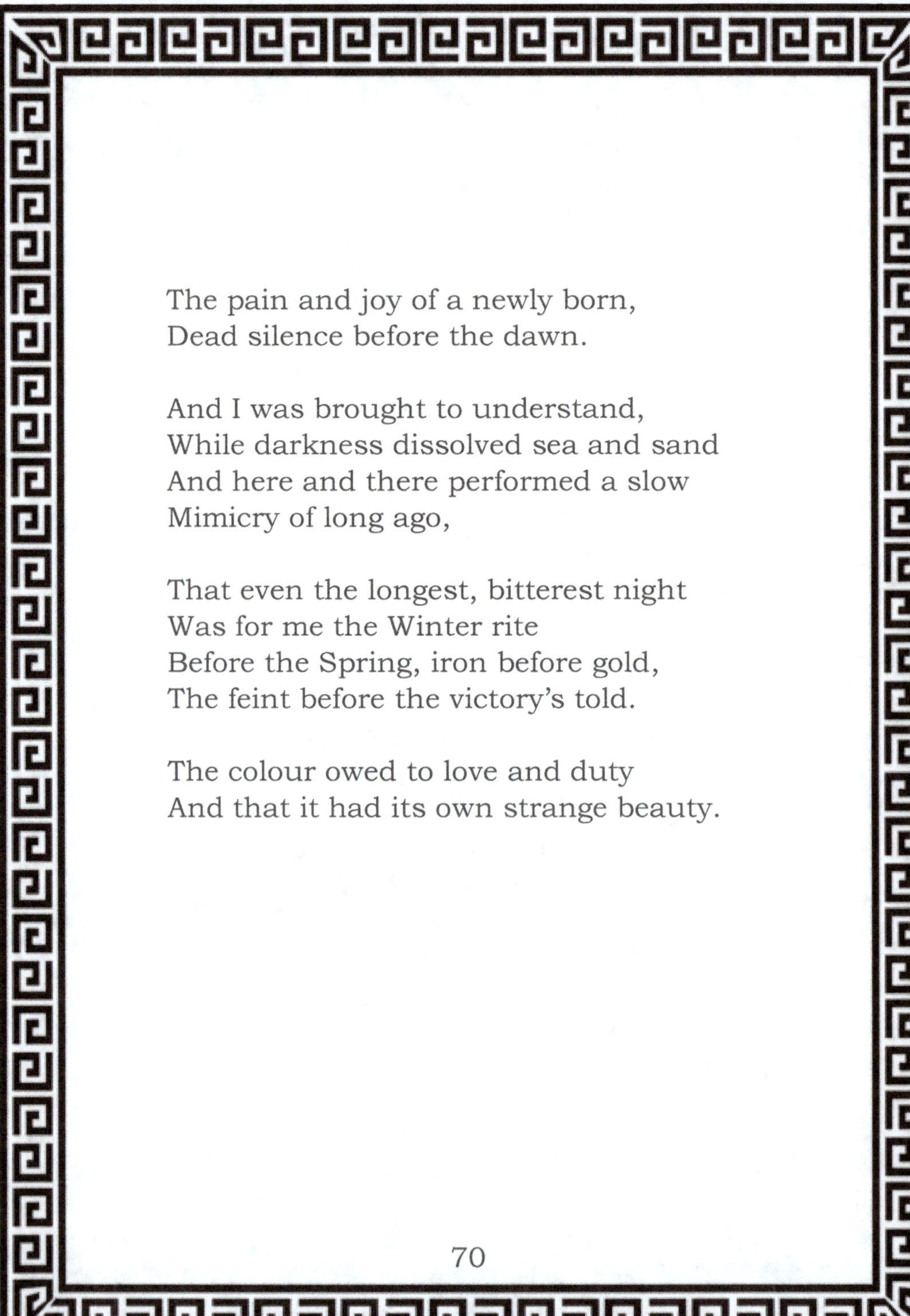

The pain and joy of a newly born,
Dead silence before the dawn.

And I was brought to understand,
While darkness dissolved sea and sand
And here and there performed a slow
Mimicry of long ago,

That even the longest, bitterest night
Was for me the Winter rite
Before the Spring, iron before gold,
The feint before the victory's told.

The colour owed to love and duty
And that it had its own strange beauty.

THE PROMISE OF SNOW

At a time when the trees
Like paper ghosts capture
Starlight, and the restless seas
Freeze along margins of rapture;

When a near universal dark
Blankets night and day
And the prospect of warm, stark
Sunlight seems so very far away,

Then the first snow falls
And the world's a quiet white,
An existential newness stalls
Dark with its own pale light.

In that season love came,
Like new snow bright with thirst,
As the brilliance of a candle flame
Burns hardest at the first.

Like a fire in the earth, a new star
In Midwinter's constellation,
The clearest, brightest light by far
Above the hubbub of our ordinary nation.

IN THE NIGHT

And God said "Let there be night"
Because he had embraced the darkness.

But the sky still shines with the clarity
Of the first morning glory,
Each star an absolute thought
Buried in oblivion,

And on her onyx throne the Moon
Weaves shadows like passing strangers
On frost-bitten trees and brittle grass,
Terrified in all the newness.

The simplicity of it was silence
So the first breath in this new world
Might just be heard. Only the rush
Of distant pebbles on a beach, falling

With the tide as if the Moon
Tyrannised still in the old world.
Something had stopped and held creation
In ice and shades of hematite.

Darkness had fallen, leaving its trace
On shadow pools and a dead, dead sea.
And we must learn to love the night
As if the Sun will never rise,

As if only the Moon's tears
Can comfort us as we blindly huddle
And fumble and fuck for warmth,
And hide our imperfections

Deep in our ischemic hearts.
Come closer, so I can lean on you.
Something new is growing there
Taking its first icy breaths.

There, where the clouds shroud the
horizon
Purple, green and blue, a rising
That is no birth, an alien sky
That doesn't know what earth this is

And that we struggle to exist. Resist,
Turn your melancholy face

Towards the Moon one last time
Before the darkness justifies

The things that we will need to know:
That fire is worth killing for,
And biting flesh transformative,
And swallowing blood a sort of quenching.

PARADISO (AFTER DANTE)

I looked up. And my eyes' clarity
Bathed more and more in that unequalled
blaze
Of light beyond the light, itself the final
truth.
And from that moment on my sight
outstripped
All powers of speech, which trembled
there
At such a spectacle, sank back, as
memory failed,
The task of painting now in words beyond
its reach.

Just like one who, half asleep, yet sees
Only the impression of a passionate
dream
And everything else is fled on the breeze,
So am I, so much of my vision gone,
And yet still my heart distils
The sweetness that was born there.
Just as the snow melts in the sun;
Just as the thoughts of the wise woman
Written on leaves are lost on the wind.

LA VITA NUOVA

THE KING OF FROGS

As she rose from the sea, new-born,
Naked on one of those first mornings,
Wringing the salt foam from her hair,
Gazing pleased on her perfect form,
She smiled and all the air about
Began to sing the world's first song
Of pure love.

And when her glistening white foot
Touched that aboriginal land
Flowers sprung up in many colours.
The trees that lined the darkened shore
Sighed for love. Animals stopped
Their grazing, curious of new
Sensations.

And from the cerulean sky
The Hours, daughters of the Sun,
Flew to clothe her in gossamer spun
From every flower on the earth
And placed upon her brow a star,
The sun's gold to circle her arms.
The first Spring

Day dawned. She made her numinous
way
To a pool of water, clear and blue,
And looked on her reflection there.
But from the woods people who came
To gaze in awe on her perfection
Seemed cold and distant, full of doubt
And hostile.

There was no love in them, their hearts
Beat only out of fearfulness.
Love, it seemed, unknown to their blood,
An alien thing, like creatures from
The deep. Love was not a word
In their vocabulary. Love
Was still born.

So, Aphrodite the Divine
For the first time in any time
Began to weep pure crystal tears,
Soft and salty like the sea
From which she'd come. Her heart

Beat sadly for humanity.
Still, she smiled.

For in the water little forms
Wriggled and danced in the light,
Struggling to reach the flower-strewn
bank
On which she stood. Their great eyes
shone,
Glistening with incipient desire.
Fingers emerged from out the spawn,
Clutching at

The rocks and reeds and mossy soil.
Great smiling mouths opened wide
To catch the sorrow flowing from
The goddess's eyes. And as the first
Of these delightful creatures bathed
In Aphrodite's tears, he was
All transformed.

His colourless body turned red and green,
A splash of yellow on his crown
Shining like topaz in the sun.
His delicate hands spreading out

To clutch her holy feet in prayer.
Gracefully she bent to take him
In her palm.

Gone the whirring tail, strong legs
Now grew to leap and dance among
The lily pads and slimy rocks,
His eyes shone blue as paradise.
And all the people roundabout
Smiled and laughed to see the crowd
Dance and sing.

But Aphrodite took this one,
Her first born, to her warm breast.
"You are my King of Frogs," she sang,
"My love, my sweetest palimpsest
On which I'll write a thousand songs
Ages to come will sing and so
Forget tears.

"Though love will be a pleasure now,
Because my bitter agony
Has watered this, a pain to all,
A longing in their burning flesh,

A crazy boiling in their blood,
Raging, leaping on the winds,
Opulence only lovers know in
Night-time cries."

The King of Frogs leapt from her hand
And dived into the watery skim.
Deep down amongst the shivering swell
A thousand colours glittered there
As all the frogs began to sing
The praise of Aphrodite, Fair
Queen of Love.

Remember this when next you see
The waters ripple in a pool
Or glassy eyes blink out at you.
We are the servants of the frogs
Who consubstantiated love,
And sang the aeons' original
Hymn of Desire.

BIRTHDAY WISHES

I hadn't really thought about you since.
The sun surprised me, that was all,
The wall of dawn had broken

And blood was bubbling in my veins,
But not because of you, the other warm
Body in the bed and my coy hard-on,

And those familiar things about the room
As well as some things new and
wonderful.
Still, I feel guilty now, a summer cheat.

Although it had been nearly thirty years
Of all remembering, like woollen yarn
Unravelling in the curtain at the window,

Letting the light in, and I sighed,
I slipped my arm around him,
And so it was the universe began.

I'd looked for you amongst the kelp
Beneath the sea. The water stung
My skin, my eyes were smeared

By eels and jellyfish. I was lost.
In underwater caverns you were
Nowhere to be found. My flesh cold,

My lungs burnt with exhalation,
Salt in my mouth, hair all tangled
And snared in weeds. You were not there.

I'd looked for you down in the earth,
Red and black, my fingers scratched,
Nails thick with it, the burning wrack

Of muscles stretched and saturated.
But you were nowhere, and I was lost.
Earth filled my eyes, my mouth,

My nostrils smelled only the decay.
My heart slowed to a falling pulse
Like a distant star murmuring

Out in space, like a bird shot through.
And there was loneliness in dying.
Then someone's hand reached down to
me.

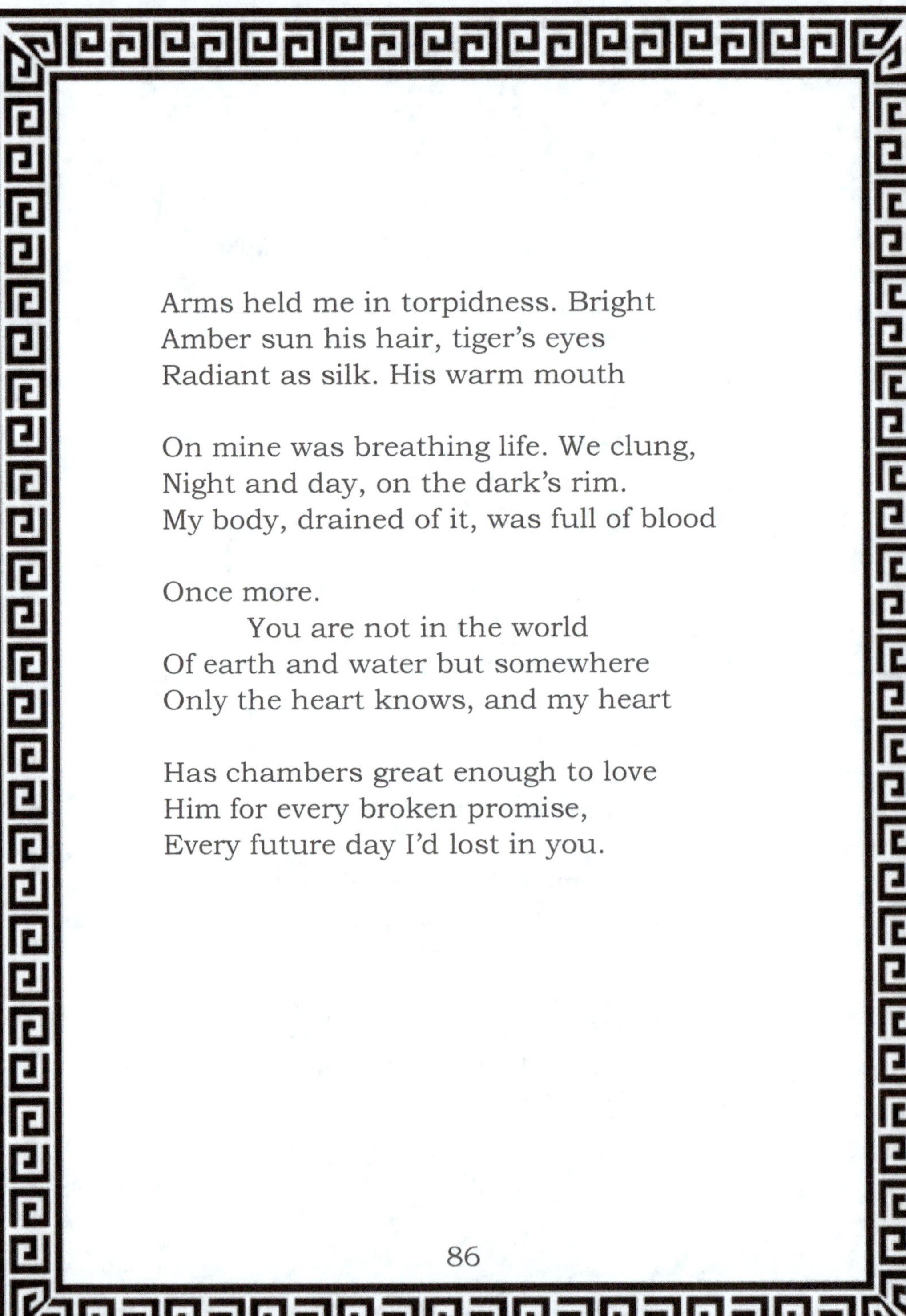

Arms held me in torpidness. Bright
Amber sun his hair, tiger's eyes
Radiant as silk. His warm mouth

On mine was breathing life. We clung,
Night and day, on the dark's rim.
My body, drained of it, was full of blood

Once more.
          You are not in the world
Of earth and water but somewhere
Only the heart knows, and my heart

Has chambers great enough to love
Him for every broken promise,
Every future day I'd lost in you.

DESIRE

Let me lie faithful to your body still
For as long as it lasts – a moment,
A lifetime of love, the edge of torment
Pleasuring your pulse and ball sack, the
spill

Of fingers over skin, the rise and fall
Of your breath. The nuzzle of my cock
Against your hole, that elemental shock
Of foraging and finding what is all.

What's hidden underneath the night,
Within the veins and sinews and beyond
The physical press, raw nerves respond
To a primitive amphetamine bite;

Feeling the glowing flow of elemental
blood
Like a torrent in a swollen dream pool,
Pound and polarize the ice cream cool
Of your tongue against the burning flood.

But give me a pitcher full of fire
And I will pour it out on you

And lick it up and pass it through
Your lips so you know how desire

Tastes; make me a channel for its heat
A falling star in the velvet night,
A cauldron seething with the fierce white
Of molten hearts, love made between
beats.

But let me lie quiet by your side for now,
The lips that burned me gentle in sleep's
fold,
The curious eyes which picked apart my
soul
Careless under the slight crease of your
brow.

Like the sunlight on the sea you draw me
in;
Like the sun breaking though clouds you
make me start;
Like a cold fountain you penetrate my
heart.
You are my religion now, the blood
beneath my skin.

WHAT THE MOON TELLS ME

Where have you gone to?
I listen to your breathing in the dead
night
When the stars are all the light
And the Moon, that great goddess,
Has hidden her silver shadows
Throughout the house. You are by me
But I do not know where you are.

Where have you gone to?
When the Sun is on the garden
And you stand, a light smile
On your lips, a golden face
That I love. But you are not with me.
And your hazel eyes are like dark stars
And I do not know where you are.

Where have you gone to?
When you are not with me
And messages are short and long in
coming,
When the distance between us

Is like a storm at sea, a broken road,
And I long for the wings of a god
Or the eyes of Argus but see nothing.

Where have you gone to?
When we fuck, and your lips are on mine.
Our tongues play with the blood
In our mouths. Your body's mine,
You are mine for the Moon tells me,
And I know there's nothing to fear
For you have gone nowhere but here.

ANIMAL CONSTELLATIONS

I could smell you
Like a trail of blood
On the snow, blue
Veins pumping a flood

Of ecstasy.
It led me to your lair
Where I can see
Black eyes shine like prayer.

Has the cruel one
Broken down the fence?
Can you still run?
Can you feel the dense

Sweet pelt on me?
I can taste your fear.
And to be free
Does my hot breath sear

Your flesh like stone
From deep in the earth?
My teeth on bone
Tear at what it's worth.

I'm not sorry
I'm not rational.
I don't worry
I'm an animal.

When love is scent,
Red in tooth and claw,
Head tumescent,
There's no moral law,

Only the wild
Instinct to be fucked
And fuck – the child
World of stroked and sucked.

And how I love
You for giving in
Though now I shove
Inside you my sin.

The dance of death
Is love, and we'll pant
Our last hard breath
Fucking till we can't.

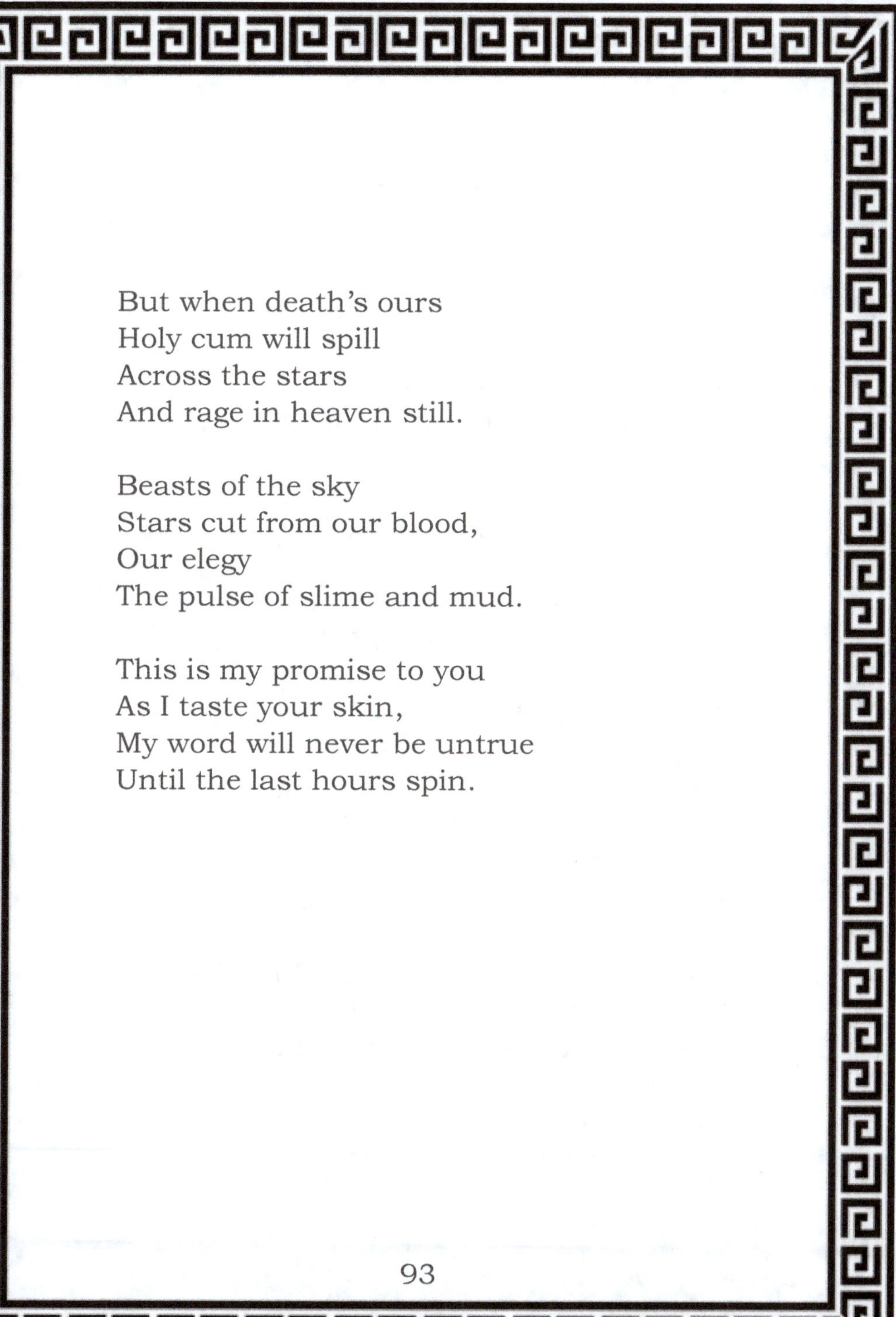

But when death's ours
Holy cum will spill
Across the stars
And rage in heaven still.

Beasts of the sky
Stars cut from our blood,
Our elegy
The pulse of slime and mud.

This is my promise to you
As I taste your skin,
My word will never be untrue
Until the last hours spin.

LETHE (AFTER BAUDELAIRE)

Rest heavy on my heart, indifferent
precious
Tiger, sweet and listless beast;
I want to snare my fingers, unreleased,
An age in the tangle of your tresses;

In your thighs, rank with your particular
scent,
I want to bury my poor aching head,
And breathe, like withered flowers on a
bed,
The sweet whiff of my love's dement.

I want to sleep! Sleep more than remain!
In a sweeter-than-death forget,
I will scatter my kisses without regret
On your body's shining copper stain.

To tranquilise my bottomless distress
There's nothing like your bed's abyss;
And Lethe dribbles through your kiss
From your mouth's prison of
forgetfulness.

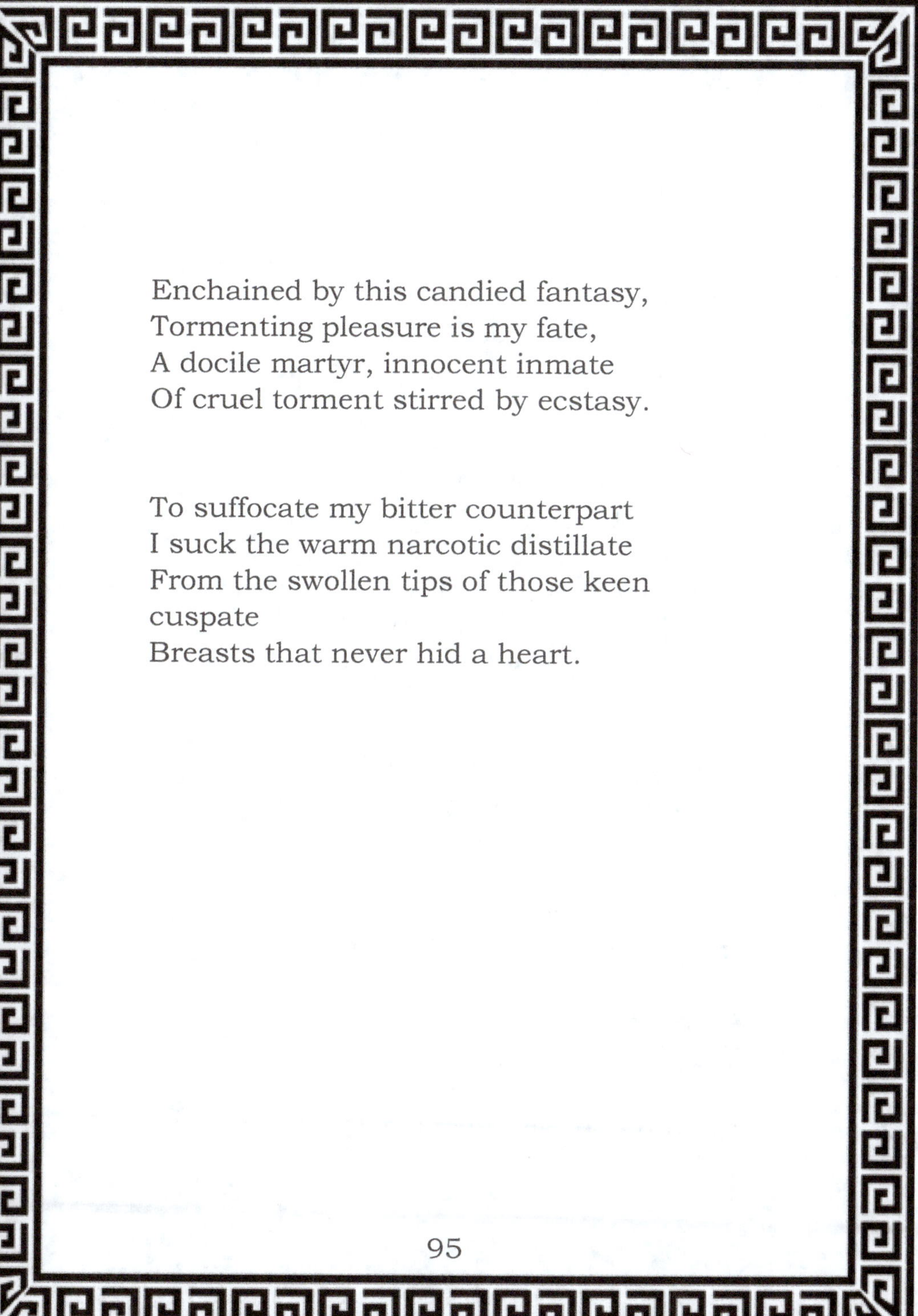

Enchained by this candied fantasy,
Tormenting pleasure is my fate,
A docile martyr, innocent inmate
Of cruel torment stirred by ecstasy.

To suffocate my bitter counterpart
I suck the warm narcotic distillate
From the swollen tips of those keen
cuspate
Breasts that never hid a heart.

CIRCE'S WAND

Set us free
For the water is cool
And we would soak our feet in it.

Set us free
For the sun on our backs
Burns like a branding iron.

We would lie in the shade
And stretch our limbs like men
Who have come a long way to be here.

Set us free
From ourselves, our animal
Natures, into the warm air

Where spirits live
Like kings among the trees
And sing beneath the brown bark.

Set us free
And we would happily be
Olive tree or falling rain,
Anything but what we are now.

TOO HAPPY (AFTER BAUDELAIRE)

Everything about you is pride
Of beauty, like a painted scene,
Laughter cools your fucking eyes
Like a chill breeze in a summer sky.

The sad-eyed stranger you brush by
Is dazzled by the insane flush
Of health that ripples all about
You, like waves on a breezy sea.

And that ridiculous splash
Of colour on your crazy clothes
Might inspire a dandied poet
With thoughts of dancing crocuses.

But all this motley show just hides
The sufferance of your vagrant heart,
Your madness only drives me mad:
I hate to love you in an instant.

Sometimes in some lovely spot
Where I will drag my listless bones
I feel with bitter irony
The sun is burning on my skin,

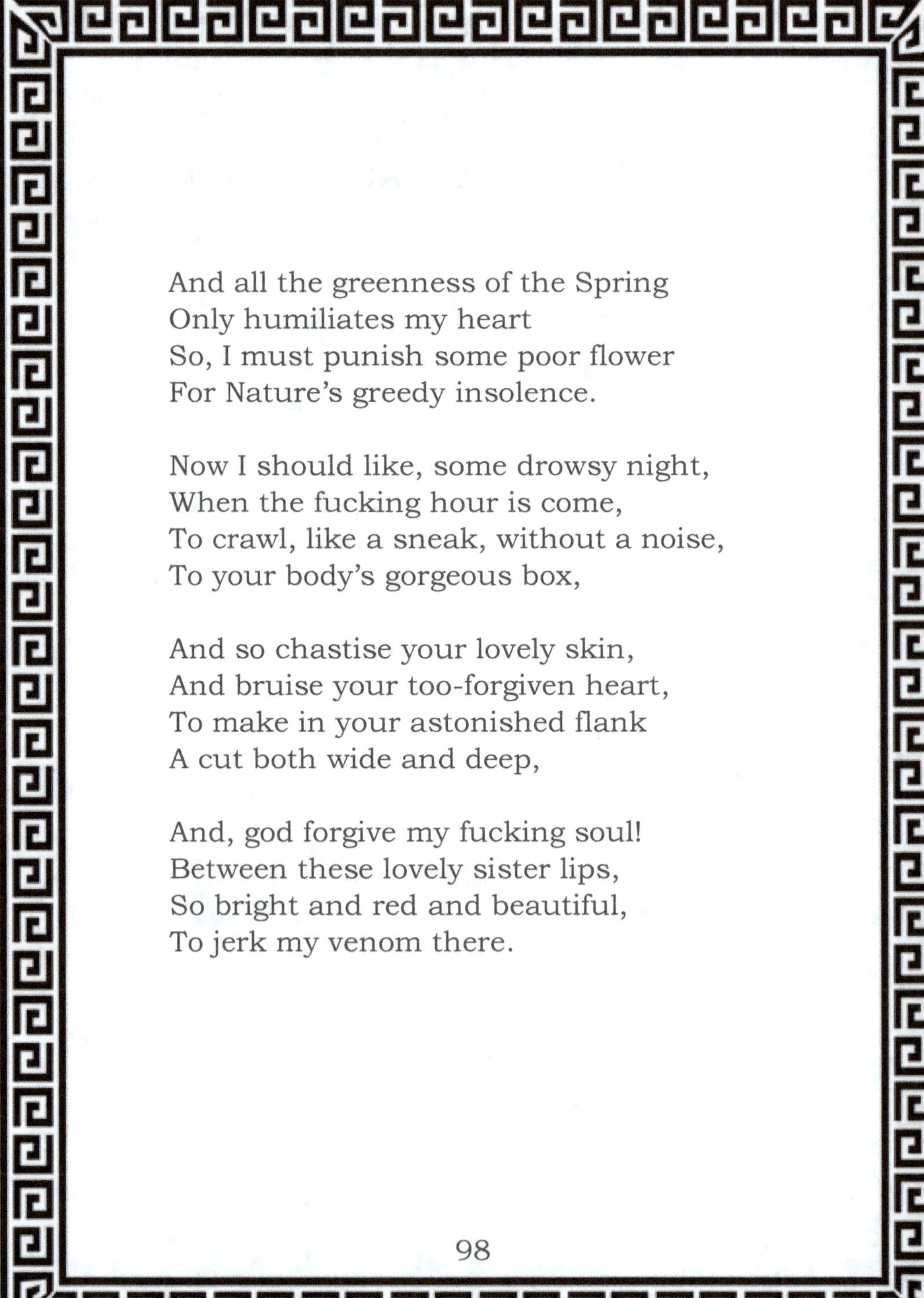

And all the greenness of the Spring
Only humiliates my heart
So, I must punish some poor flower
For Nature's greedy insolence.

Now I should like, some drowsy night,
When the fucking hour is come,
To crawl, like a sneak, without a noise,
To your body's gorgeous box,

And so chastise your lovely skin,
And bruise your too-forgiven heart,
To make in your astonished flank
A cut both wide and deep,

And, god forgive my fucking soul!
Between these lovely sister lips,
So bright and red and beautiful,
To jerk my venom there.

WATER SPRITE

Soft air and the early summer heat
That pricked the back of your bare neck
Makes sweat spring up, the sweet
Smell of a man, pheromonal fleck
Of warm body and strong blood beat.

The bluebell woods pioneer
An electric blue melody.
And doves whisper in your ear
"Follow me, follow me,"
The sound of earth's gyring gear.

Now to a stretch of deep-water blue
Down sun-wrung rocks they fly,
You climb and fall, the sheen shines
through,
Sheer as a looking glass, dazzling sky
And larksong and rocks and you.

Steep walls of granite like muscles flexing
And in the pool a ripple bursts –

Dark gold hair, blue eyes, a smile
reflecting
Your own – your body's primitive thirsts
For cool and heat and some other
expecting.

And you can't drop that sky-blue gaze.
Stripping you wade to the sweet recoil
Of cold on flesh and let it graze
Your hot skin and wash the sweet spoil
Of sweat from you. A new world stays.

"Come closer," it's a voice you must obey.
He circles then dives and slides unseen
Beneath the glassy breakaway.
Is that his cool tongue that glides between
Your crack or just the water's play?

A patch of rising warmth, do lips
Encircle now your growing cock?
A finger, or is it a bubble, slips
Inside your warm hole, the lock
Of deep-throat hands upon your hips?

You're lifted from the glowing pool,
He coils and winds about you now
His breath on your hot neck is cool
His cock's a deep insistent plough
Stretching your hole with feral drool.

The larks are numbing the electric sky.
The sun dries up the splash of dew
And with preternatural sighs
He pours himself inside of you
His mouth is yours, his arms, his chest,
his thighs.

A moment passes. He seems to drain,
The weight of flesh is liquid light,
Only your body remembers his stain.
Your pulse quickens, your skin's tension
tight,
Your hole twitches with the memory of
pain.

"Hey!" The sun blazes, you look up in
surprise,

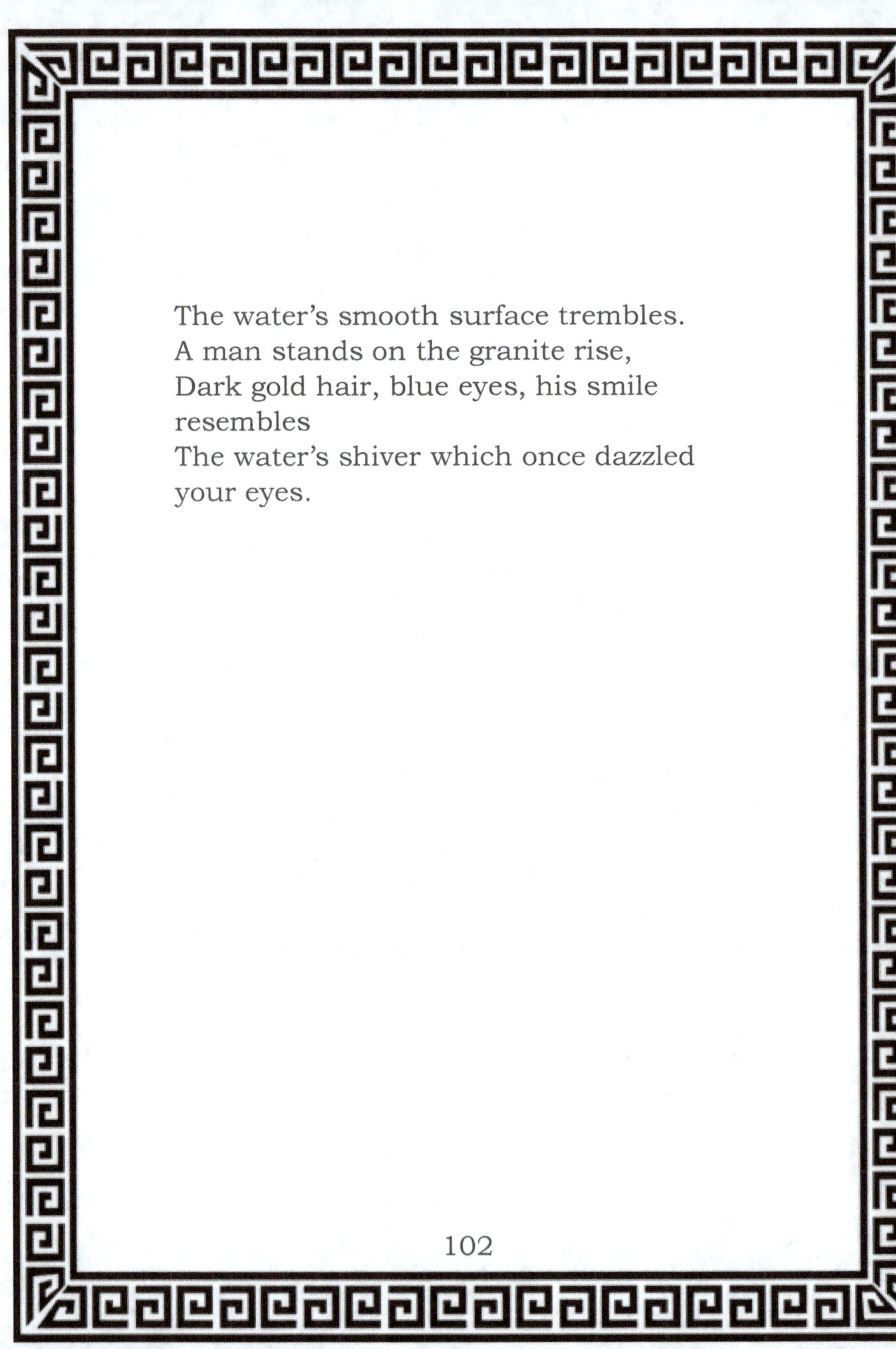

The water's smooth surface trembles.
A man stands on the granite rise,
Dark gold hair, blue eyes, his smile resembles
The water's shiver which once dazzled your eyes.

THE MIRROR

As I lie with you on our bed
The sheet all wrapped around us
Like a crumpled veil, Venus
Has made a crown of your hair,
You head pale and shadowy.

There's nothing of your body
Except what my fingers touch,
Only a face on a silver radiance
Of sleep. Don't open those eyes
Yet. I'm not awake enough
For their enchantment.

And I dare not look back
For fear of you dissolving into air
With nothing but your eyes, your lips
Whispering goodbyes.
I still remember the taste
Of blood on those lips,
The sticky perfume on your skin.

Will you dance for me? The night
Is full of love, the New Moon
Has drawn her veil of stars
To watch your feet as they move
Like serpents on the shining floor.

Dance for me and I'll
Give you what you desire:
My head upon a silver plate;
You can run your fingers through
My slime-matted hair and kiss
The bitter love on my cold mouth,
Drink the blood from my neck
And bite my lips with your teeth.

And all the world will watch
On phones and tablets and laptop
screens.
Only dance for me. And they
Will see the veils drop from the sky.

Paint your kohl-black eyes and dye
Your hands and feet with henna.

Let the sweat of your body shimmer
Like jewels in the flickering light
From a million screenshots
In honour of the great goddess.

Dance for me as you have done
Two thousand years or more,
Man, woman, demi-god,
Sex-shifter, like the blind necromancer.

I am your bloodied prophet now,
My voice is a storm
On the vast ocean,
And my desert of a heart
Will open up and swallow you
To the last, glistening drop.
My eyes will shatter
Into broken glass
Upon the floor. Your feet
Will bleed on the razor-sharp shards.
My hair will fill your mouth,
Serpent-like and poison your veins.
My cock will tear the shining veils
From off your burning flesh.

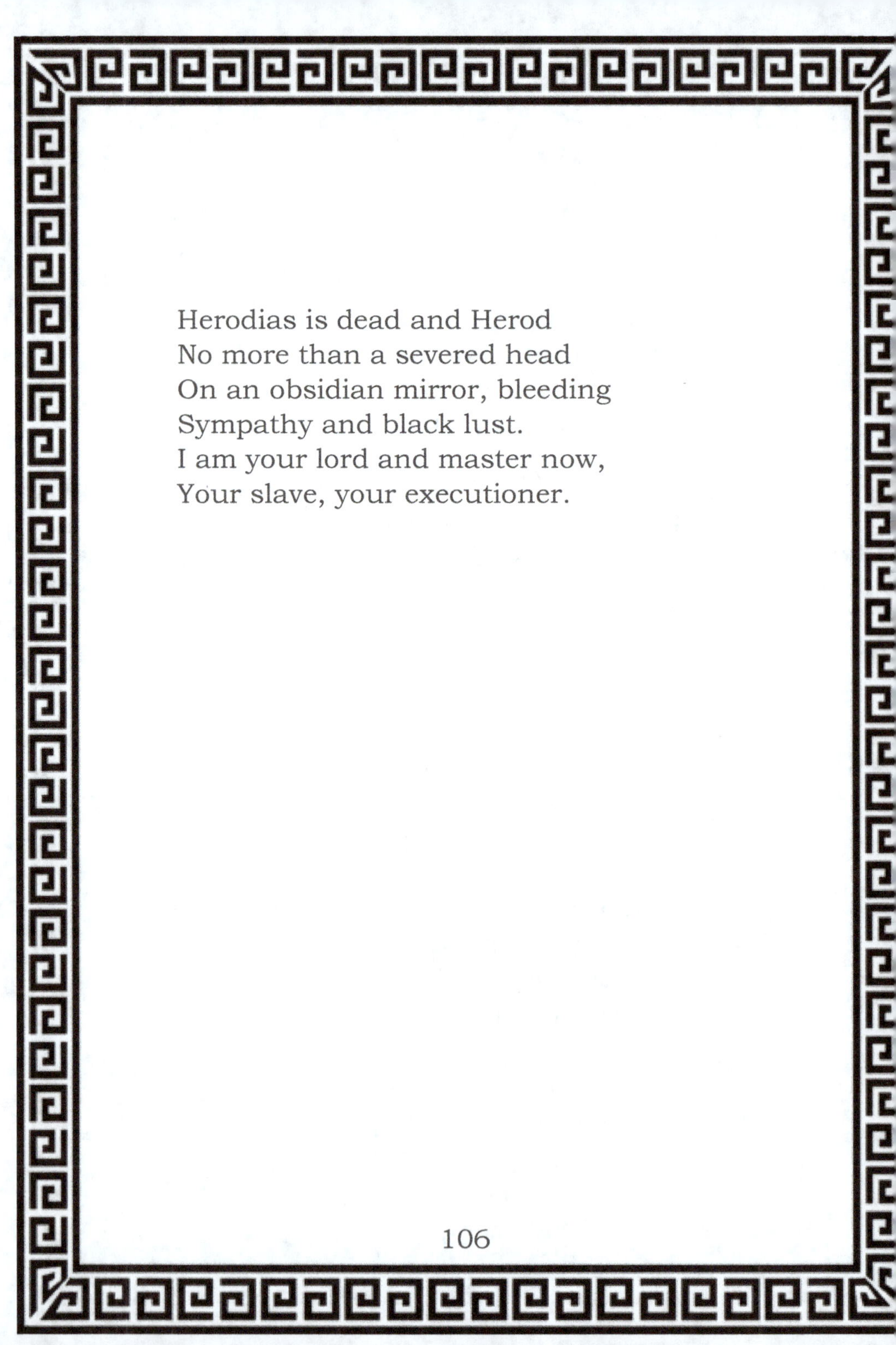

Herodias is dead and Herod
No more than a severed head
On an obsidian mirror, bleeding
Sympathy and black lust.
I am your lord and master now,
Your slave, your executioner.

EPIGRAPH

FINAL PRAYER

Come with me now, god of the woods,
Let's walk together a little way
I'll listen to your tales and play
Lover to your raging blood's

Immortal ecstasy. I'll be
The one whose body you adored
While his lips, tentative, explored
Your pipes for perfect melody.

I'll echo each beloved word
Just to feel your warm voice tremble
In my flesh and disassemble
Every rock and tree and bird

That flies up, and all living out
Their lives, creeping, crawling, on the
earth.
I'll be the terror given birth
In human hearts with your great shout.

I'll fill my veins with blood and free
The pale corpse your witchy handmaid

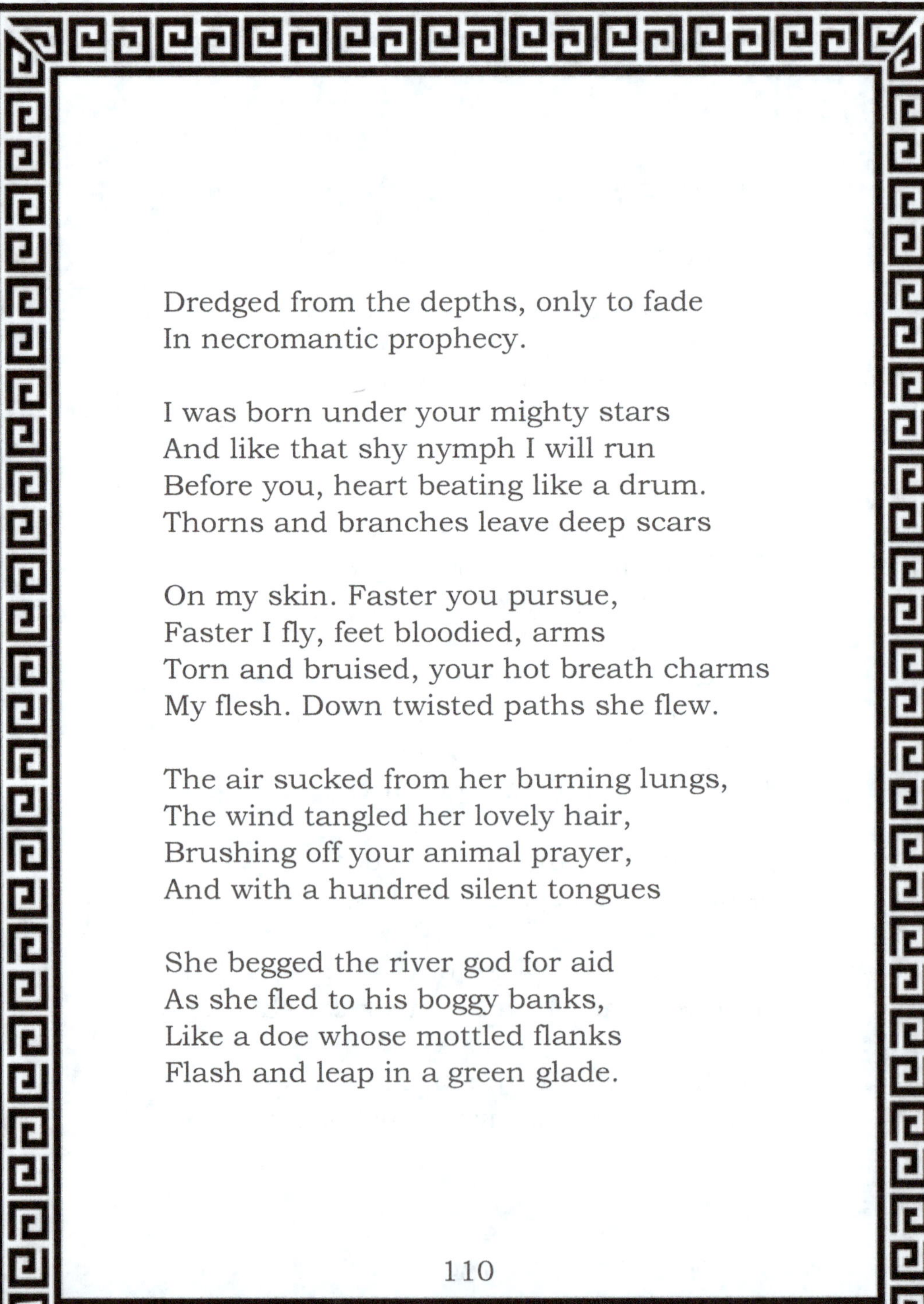

Dredged from the depths, only to fade
In necromantic prophecy.

I was born under your mighty stars
And like that shy nymph I will run
Before you, heart beating like a drum.
Thorns and branches leave deep scars

On my skin. Faster you pursue,
Faster I fly, feet bloodied, arms
Torn and bruised, your hot breath charms
My flesh. Down twisted paths she flew.

The air sucked from her burning lungs,
The wind tangled her lovely hair,
Brushing off your animal prayer,
And with a hundred silent tongues

She begged the river god for aid
As she fled to his boggy banks,
Like a doe whose mottled flanks
Flash and leap in a green glade.

Teach me to run until I fall.
I will not turn, I will not hide,
I will not treacherously slide
Among the reeds or weakly call

My father just to be transformed.
I'd happily submit and feel
Your body randomly conceal,
Make each atom of me re-formed.

Great god, of whom the ancients lied
When they pronounced you were no more;
Whoever whispered from the shore,
It wasn't you they said had died.

As long as earth trembles and streams
Flow fast among the ever green
Valleys, heard but never seen,
Still, you will animate our dreams.

And we will worship you among
The rocks, leave offerings beneath
The trees, and soothe our mortal griefs
With your sweet everlasting song.

Great god of all, master of strife,
Lord of pleasure, hunter of night
And master of the day, the light
Of she who brought me back to life.

Make me one with the teeming sea
And blend me with the deep red earth,
Cut me, mould me, make my blood worth
The tremor of your ecstasy.

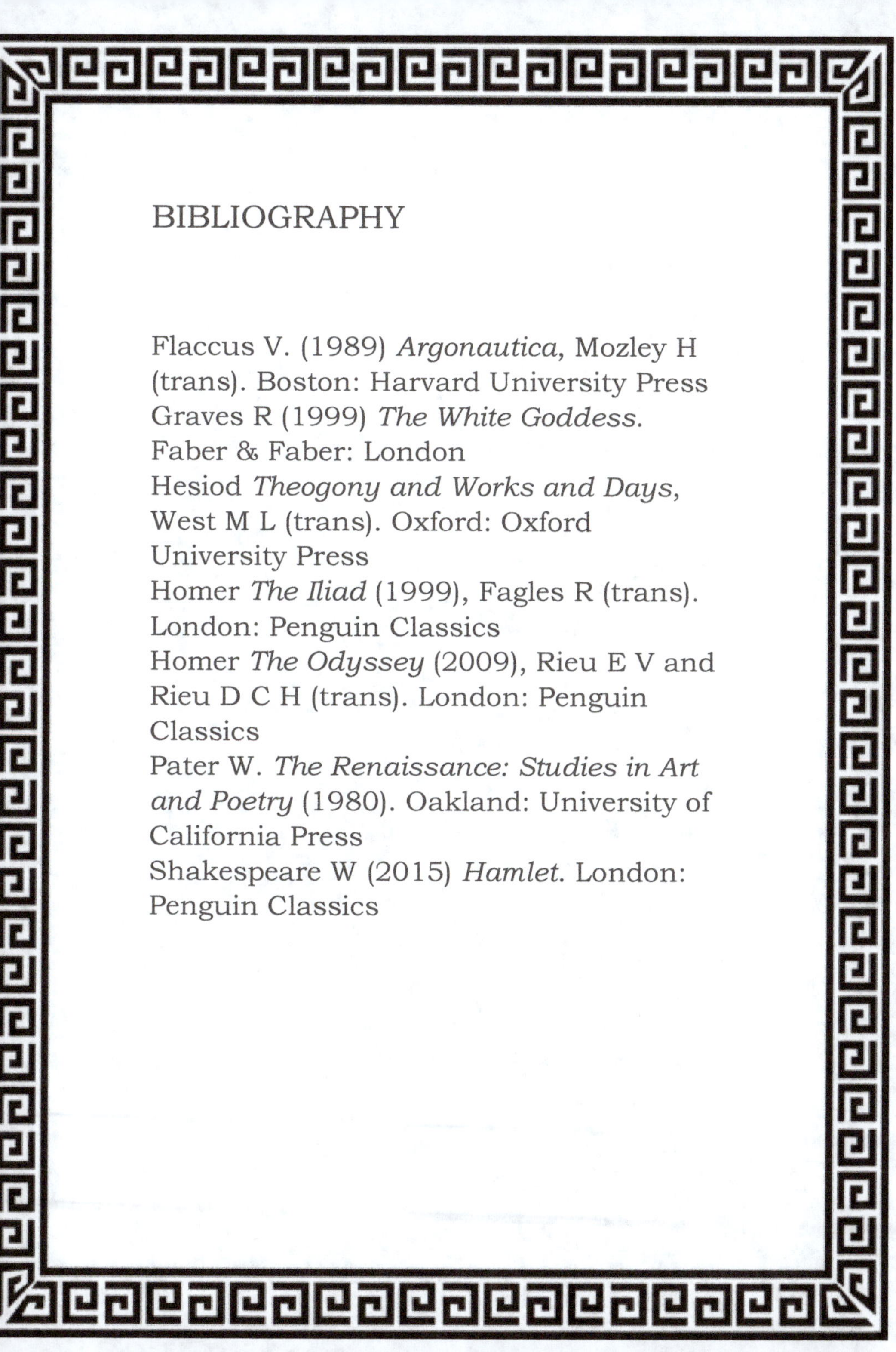

BIBLIOGRAPHY

Flaccus V. (1989) *Argonautica*, Mozley H (trans). Boston: Harvard University Press

Graves R (1999) *The White Goddess*. Faber & Faber: London

Hesiod *Theogony and Works and Days*, West M L (trans). Oxford: Oxford University Press

Homer *The Iliad* (1999), Fagles R (trans). London: Penguin Classics

Homer *The Odyssey* (2009), Rieu E V and Rieu D C H (trans). London: Penguin Classics

Pater W. *The Renaissance: Studies in Art and Poetry* (1980). Oakland: University of California Press

Shakespeare W (2015) *Hamlet*. London: Penguin Classics

Kevin Childs is a writer and lecturer in the history of art. He has written extensively for The Independent, The Times and Huffington Post. Kevin has also been a screenwriter on various film and television projects. *Metamorphosis* is his first collection of poetry.